PRINCIPLED
PROFITS

OUTWARD
SUCCESS
— IS AN —
INSIDE JOB

BOBBY ALBERT

NEW YORK

NASHVILLE • MELBOURNE • VANCOUVER

PRINCIPLED PROFITS

Published in New York, New York, by Morgan James Publishing. Morgan James is a trademark of Morgan James, LLC.
www.MorganJamesPublishing.com

The Morgan James Speakers Group can bring authors to your live event. For more information or to book an event visit The Morgan James Speakers Group at www.TheMorganJamesSpeakersGroup.com.

ISBN 978-1-68350-543-3 paperback
ISBN 978-1-68350-544-0 eBook
Library of Congress Control Number: 2017905639

Cover Design by:
Alex Tibio

Cover Layout & Interior Design by:
Megan Whitney
Creative Ninja Designs
megan@creativeninjadesigns.com

In an effort to support local communities, raise awareness and funds, Morgan James Publishing donates a percentage of all book sales for the life of each book to Habitat for Humanity Peninsula and Greater Williamsburg.

Get involved today! Visit
www.MorganJamesBuilds.com

This book is dedicated to my wife, Susan, whose support and friendship I have enjoyed for forty-three years and counting, and to our three sons, Rob, Brian, and Kyle, of whom I'm very proud and who are my life's legacy.

TABLE OF CONTENTS

Introduction   1

Part I: Leading and Managing   7

Chapter One: Are You a Leader or a Manager?   9

Define Your Leadership as You Discover the Differences Between Leading and Managing

Chapter Two: The Fastest Way to Improve Your Leadership   33

Leverage Your Leadership as You Value and Empower People

Part II: Process and Content   57

Chapter Three: Embrace the *How* as You Pursue the *What*   59

Transform Your Leadership by Adopting the Principle of Process and Content

Part III: Principle vs. Expediency   85

Chapter Four: Direction Trumps Speed   87

Direct Your Leadership by Employing a Principled Approach to Business and Life

Chapter Five: A Mindset That Creates Success   105

Energize Your Leadership with an Abundance Mindset

Part IV: Core Values   **113**

Chapter Six: Discover and Build Your Core   115

Center Your Leadership on Your Core Values for Extraordinary Results

Chapter Seven: Your Great Ideas Will Die, Unless . . .   145

Amplify Your Leadership as You Convey Your Core Values

Part V: Workplace Culture   **173**

Chapter Eight: Great Leaders Don't Focus on Culture   175

Focus Your Leadership on the Fundamentals, and the Right Culture Will Follow

Chapter Nine: Serve Your People, Strengthen Your Culture   201

Employ Your Leadership to Serve Others and Enhance Your Workplace Culture

Part VI: Goals and Controls   **225**

Chapter Ten: Tap the Power of Goals   227

Fuel Your Leadership Through Collaborative Goal Setting

Chapter Eleven: A Powerful Way to Unite and Inspire Your Team   251

Perpetuate Your Leadership by Setting Goals and Monitoring Progress

Conclusion   285

Acknowledgements   289

About the Author   291

Resources   293

INTRODUCTION

THE BEST EMPLOYERS IN THE U.S. SAY THEIR GREATEST TOOL IS _____.

T he above headline caught my attention. It was the title of an article appearing in *Forbes* that featured the characteristics of the top one hundred places to work in the United States.[1]

I'll fill in the missing word to complete the headline in a moment, but I'd like to ask you: What word or words would you jot in that blank? You might suggest "Big Data" or "Social Media" or "High Wages." Each of these options reflects a rational ending to the above headline—but all of them miss the mark!

OK, it's time to fill in the blank. The headline revealed that the best employers say their greatest tool is *culture*. The article stated, "The best employers are better because more business leaders are focused on workplace culture as a competitive tool." In fact, the authors go on to reveal, "Google's leaders explicitly attribute the company's financial performance to its benevolent people practices."

---

[1] Milton Moskowitz and Robert Levering, "The Best Employers in the U.S. Say Their Greatest Tool Is Culture," *Fortune*, March 5, 2015, *http://fortune.com/2015/03/05/best-companies-greatest-tool-is-culture*.

You might be thinking, *"It's a dog-eat-dog world out there! I'm simply trying to stay afloat. I'm constantly dealing with interpersonal problems within my team. My competitors are lowering their prices. I'm just trying to make payroll next week! What is so special and important about culture?"*

Well, the proof is in the pudding, as my mother used to say. According to a study by the Russell Investment Group, since 1998, the "100 Best Companies to Work For" have outperformed the S&P 500 Index by a ratio of nearly two to one. I don't know about you, but when I read about a two-to-one advantage in business, I sit up and take notice!

If building a great workplace culture is so instrumental to extraordinary success, then why don't more companies do it? One reason is that cultivating an award-winning culture is easier to discuss than to achieve.

Many leaders are comfortable focusing on such goals as increasing sales by 25 percent or decreasing overhead by 10 percent. But ask them to significantly improve their workplace culture, and they start staring out the window with a blank look on their faces. Even defining workplace culture seems like pie-in-the-sky leadership. And who has time for that?

Perhaps we should consider a related question: Who has time to double their performance as compared to the S&P 500? When the question is posed in that way, we become keenly interested in the idea of creating a dynamic, award-winning culture, don't we?

Let's look at some statistics related to the survival of new businesses in the United States:

About half of all new establishments survive five years or more and about one-third survive 10 years or more. As one would expect, the probability of survival increases with a firm's age. Survival rates have changed little over time. (US Bureau of Labor Statistics, Business Employment Dynamics)

Only about one-third of new businesses survive ten years or more—pretty sobering, when you think about it. And we're not talking thriving and growing; we are just referring to survival—i.e., simply unlocking the door to your business on Monday morning and flipping over the "Sorry, We're Closed" sign to reveal that "Yes, We're Open" so folks know you still have a pulse!

Statistics like this underscore the importance of doing all we can, as leaders, to shepherd and grow our businesses. So, back to this idea of workplace culture. When we run across a key finding that reveals a common trait shared by the best of the best, it's time to "go to school" and learn all we can.

My own leadership journey eventually led me to build and grow a company with a strong, inspiring workplace culture. Starting at the ripe old age of twenty, I learned and stretched and grew my leadership. The company had ups and downs, but I resolved to keep growing and learning—even (or perhaps especially) from my mistakes.

My father's untimely death thrust the reins of his small business of five employees into my unproven young hands. Some thirty-eight years later, I sold our company of over 150 employees and effectively passed the reins along to the next generation of leadership.

Although I did not know it at the time, I had discovered some concrete, repeatable steps to building the organizational culture that most leaders strive for. I'd uncovered principles that became the foundation upon which our dynamic, engaged workplace grew.

If you desire to have a better culture, may I suggest that the pursuit of it should *not* be your focus? No, that is not a typo. The surest way to achieve the culture that you want is to focus on something else! And that "something else" is comprised of the principles that form the foundation of a values-driven culture.

They don't teach these principles in business school, but when I went to the "school of business," I discovered, refined, and lived out the power of these truths:

- *The important (and different) roles of leading and managing.* When you understand the differences between leading and managing and recognize which role you naturally lean toward, it becomes easier to take the next step in your journey of development.

- *An understanding of process and content.* This involves viewing all of our actions through the powerful filters of "what" we say and do (content) and "how" we say and do it (process).

- *The differences between principled and expedient decision making.* Want to experience better results? Make better decisions. Want to make better decisions? Learn the stark contrasts between principled and expedient ways of thinking and living.

- *The cornerstone of core values.* When you know your core values, everything changes. One of the top priorities for any leader is to identify, communicate, and live out his or her core values—personally and corporately.

- *Key areas of cultural focus—a scorecard for your culture.* What does a great, inspiring workplace culture really look like? It turns out that model workplaces have several key characteristics. As you develop your leadership and values, this section can serve as a map to guide you to the right improvements.

- *Maintained momentum through goals and controls.* Once your business and culture are headed in the right direction, there are proven methods to help you maintain and even accelerate your momentum.

It took me years of asking questions, of seeking and learning, to fully understand and implement the principles I am about to share with you. My hope and prayer is that you, fellow leader, will grow and develop yourself, your organization, and your culture far faster and with more confidence through these values-driven principles than you ever could by vainly striving for a better culture.

The results of this approach in my own company were nothing short of transformational. We assembled a unified team of professionals that served our customers, suppliers, and even ourselves with passion and excellence. This resulted in extraordinary growth—500 percent in revenue and profits—during one of our country's toughest economic downturns.

This book represents the deepest, most fundamental, and most transformative business truths that I know. I encourage you to read it actively, with pen and highlighter in hand. Identify and emphasize passages that speak to you, and record the thoughts that bubble up as you read. True growth and transformation is a process, and your personalized marks will help you more effectively revisit these words as time goes by.

I've also positioned many "Pause for Reflection" prompts throughout the book, and I encourage you to pause and think deeply about your responses to the questions listed. Consider using this book as a text for your next leadership-team book review. The questions can serve as conversation starters to guide a deeper discovery process with your team.

As I imagine you reading this introduction, I'm energized with anticipation of what this book could mean to you. Learning and applying the principles that follow will most certainly set you on a path to greater performance and purpose—in both business and life!

Outward success is an inside job.

PART I
LEADING AND MANAGING

CHAPTER ONE:
Are You a Leader or a Manager?

DEFINE YOUR LEADERSHIP AS YOU DISCOVER THE DIFFERENCES BETWEEN LEADING AND MANAGING

"Management is doing things right; leadership is doing the right things."

PETER F. DRUCKER

T here's a great difference between leading *people* and managing *things*.

One requires a strategic focus on effective communication and relationships. The other requires a tactical focus on efficient processes and systems. Both leadership *and* management are necessary to produce healthy and thriving organizations.

All too often, though, relationships play second fiddle to results. I imagine you're thinking, "I *do* listen to and respect my people. I really value their input." That is exactly what I thought about my own leadership for many years. And I, like you, sincerely thought I was doing well in the relationship department—until I received an evaluation.

In 1989, through an anonymous 360-degree evaluation, I learned that many of the people around me thought I could *significantly* improve in terms of relationships. Ouch! I learned that while I was sincere—I was courteous and respectful when employees wanted to communicate something to me—I did not really seek out, listen to, and learn from my people's insights and advice.

Insight: The more you elevate relationships, the more you will benefit from the improved results that only a truly valued and united team can deliver!

I began searching for ways to increase my knowledge and improve my communication style, ultimately learning several practical ways to move my leadership from just *knowing* to actually *doing*. Based on my research and interactions in the workplace, I developed methods that truly strengthened our workplace relationships. This intentional focus on people, in turn, created a dynamic team that achieved the results I had always desired.

Effective leaders allow (and even train) their people to learn, grow, and contribute to the organization in meaningful ways. They also allow their people to help them learn through open and honest feedback.

You should endeavor to connect with your peers and employees even if you *think* you're already doing so. There are immediate and invaluable advantages to building and enhancing your workplace relationships. By now, you may be wondering whether you should make some changes to your own thoughts and actions regarding your workplace communication and leadership. If you are anything like me, you probably have some room for improvement!

Insight: I learned that there is a big difference between being nice and being an effective leader.

Here's the good news: you don't have to change your entire leadership strategy overnight. You can begin by implementing small changes and go from there based on responses and feedback.

You will need to determine whether your natural bent, or bias, is toward leading or managing and examine the differences between the two—and understand the benefits of pursuing excellence in both relationships *and* results. These tasks are the purpose of this chapter.

The result of these approaches has been nothing short of transformational in my company and in my leadership. You can experience the very same shift in your organization and leadership—starting today.

Discover Your Bent

As a young boy growing up in colonial Virginia, skipping stones across the Rappahannock River, George Washington seemed like no one special. Countless others had greater wealth or connections. Yet even at an early age, he had a bent—a natural leaning, a propensity—that was recognized by others. Ultimately, his bent toward courage and leadership resulted in his appointment as commander of the Continental Army during the Revolutionary War, as well as his unanimous election to the office of president (twice).

We all have a bent, or bias, toward thinking and acting a certain way. Our bents typically develop throughout childhood, driven by our character and natural abilities, which is one of many reasons why, as parents, we have a responsibility to help our children understand and appropriately use their life's bent.

By adulthood, we usually have a good idea of where our strengths and weaknesses lie. This applies to the business world as clearly as to any other area of life. In business, I've found that there are two main leanings: leading and managing.

It's not as difficult as you might think to determine which way you lean. You can better understand your bent by answering the following seven questions, each of which is general in nature and has two response options.

Move quickly through the questions—you need to be authentic. Your response is *not* what you aspire to be like or what you think sounds good. Rather, your response is simply a way to view who you are at this moment.

CIRCLE A OR B FOR EACH QUESTION BELOW.

1. **What would you rather do?**

    A. Analyze the details of today's tasks.

    B. Dream about your vision for the future.

2. **How are you more likely to spend your time?**

    A. Optimizing current systems and processes.

    B. Looking for new opportunities.

3. **What are you more focused on?**

    A. Accomplishing a specific assignment.

    B. Establishing and building relationships.

4. **How do you more frequently act?**

    A. Reactively respond to changes as they occur.

    B. Proactively look for and study changing trends.

5. **Which do you prefer?**

   A. The safety of a calm harbor.

   B. High-risk, sometimes unpredictable situations.

6. **When you make decisions, which do you depend on more?**

   A. Facts and figures.

   B. What your instinct or gut tells you.

7. **What do you enjoy?**

   A. Preserving the current processes and procedures.

   B. Innovating and creating new products or services.

Now tally how many A's and how many B's you have. If your answers leaned toward the A's, it means your bent is toward management. If your answers leaned toward the B's, it means your bent is toward leadership.

If you are one of those whose answers are about equally A and B, it does not mean you are ideally balanced between leading and managing. In reality, we all need to be stronger in both areas. Let's say you answered the first question above with a B. This means you can grow your effectiveness by intentionally learning the skills and behaviors associated with the complementary answer A for that question. The best combination is to employ both leading *and* managing qualities in our daily work.

When I answered these questions, I chose B every time! In fact, looking back to my childhood, my leaning has always been toward leading. Over the years, though, I've learned many of the skills reflected by the A answers, which has allowed me to become a more well-rounded person—whether leading or managing.

In the same way, you may look back on your younger years and discover that your natural tendency has been prevalent since childhood. You would also be wise to observe your bent, work to improve the skills needed to offset your natural bias toward either leading or managing, and surround yourself with people who possess skills that complement yours. When we all work together, the results exceed anything we can accomplish on our own.

Although "leadership" has a nobler connotation than "management," please remember: each role or tendency is neither *better* nor *higher* than the other. They are equally important and necessary for an organization to excel. Furthermore, great leaders and great managers need each other to maximize their potential. Leaders and managers make excellent teammates.

Leaders without managers cannot keep what they grow, and managers without leaders cannot grow what they keep! —JOHN C. MAXWELL

Whether your bent is toward leading or managing, you can become more effective by learning the skills at the other end of the spectrum.

Pause for Reflection:

1. *Would you categorize yourself as more of a leader, a manager, or an equal mix of both?*

2. *If you scored very strongly as either a leader or manager, how can you begin to make small changes in your daily routine to incorporate the skills and traits of the other role?*

3. *Consider using my Leadership Identity Assessment, which offers detailed feedback based on your assessment score: BobbyAlbert.com/LeadershipIdentity.*

The Difference Between Leading and Managing

When my father unexpectedly died in 1973, I was twenty years old and a recent university graduate. I immediately became not only the breadwinner in our family but also the new leader of our small family business. To further complicate matters, I discovered the five-employee business was carrying $70,000 in debt and produced less than $90,000 in annual revenue.

With the help of numerous wonderful people over many years, I grew our small, debt-laden company into a highly successful organization with over 150 employees. However, as our business grew, I had to tackle the new challenge of both leading and developing a team of leaders. Over time, I came to understand that there is a difference between approaches focused on relationships and those focused on results. I realized that this difference was a defining characteristic for leading and managing.

The following chart contrasts some of the high-level distinctions between leading and managing.

Leading	Managing
We enhance *relationships*.	We drive for *results*.
The focus is on *people*.	The focus is on *things*.
We lead *people*.	We manage *things*.
The focus is on *how* we say and do.	The focus is on *what* we say and do.

Managers and leaders have different approaches. After approximately fifteen years of using the seven-question survey from the previous section, I've seen that most people's leaning is toward managing. Regardless of your bent, the key to becoming truly effective is for managers to learn the skills of leading and for leaders to learn the skills of good management. You can better understand these two approaches by examining the following six examples. As you read through them, keep these points in mind:

- Managers are driven toward immediate results (*what* they say and do).

- Leaders are oriented toward relationships and long-term effectiveness (*how* they say and do it).

1. **With a Manager Mindset:** You make decisions based on your own high levels of knowledge and experience.

   With a Leader Mindset: You seek input from others who may have additional or different views and insights.

2. **With a Manager Mindset:** You might oversee engineers to design a product that works well but may be difficult to build, service, or repair and does not reflect the changing interests of customers and prospects.

   With a Leader Mindset: You guide the engineers to seek predesign advice from teams of customers, prospects, and employees from other departments.

3. **With a Manager Mindset:** You interview prospective employees using questions about *what* the prospects have done without exploring *how* they approached their work and *why* they made certain decisions.

   With a Leader Mindset: You ask questions about *what* the prospect has done but more extensively use follow-up questions about *how* and *why* in order to gain insights to the applicant's core values and style.

4. **With a Manager Mindset:** You simply order someone to close the door.

   With a Leader Mindset: You ask, "Could you close the door?" or "How about closing the door?"

5. **With a Manager Mindset:** As a parent or coach, you shout opinionated criticism in public about your student athlete's performance.

   With a Leader Mindset: You publicly support and encourage your athlete by constructively looking forward to opportunity, not backward to blame.

6. **With a Manager Mindset:** You provide employees with information on a "need to know" basis.

   With a Leader Mindset: You openly and respectfully provide employees with information of potential interest regarding all aspects of the organization in order to enhance their overall awareness and sense of belonging.

Do you see the difference between the drive for results versus the desire to maintain and enhance relationships? The key to becoming the most effective in your position is to maintain a healthy tension between managing for results (the *what*) while actively enhancing relationships (the *how*).

In the next section, we'll continue to explore the differences between these two approaches to getting things done and how they play out in the workplace—and with customers as well as suppliers.

Pause for Reflection:

1. *Do you know someone who is a great manager? What about an exemplary leader?*

2. *What qualities do these people display?*

3. *Are you ready to commit to becoming more effective?*

The Person or the Path

Have you ever played the airport game? On a recent trip, my flight was delayed, and then they changed the gate. My flight was then delayed again and finally cancelled. I waited in line for an hour to speak with an agent and then another thirty minutes at the counter, but neither of the two agents made eye contact with me. They never even looked up! I finally stepped as close as I could and asked them about the poor customer service. The agents' responses? One said, "This is not my flight." The other said, "I have a job to do." I eventually rented a car and drove home, which was both expensive and time-consuming. Needless to say, the airline did not make a good impression.

The whole experience left me thinking about the problem behind the problem at this airline. You see, I can almost assure you that the manager of these agents fails to emphasize and model the importance of customer service. In turn, the agents display no compassion for others. Nor do they care about providing good customer service since they don't see that behavior modeled at work.

> Everything rises and falls on leadership.
> —JOHN C. MAXWELL

It's common for managers to focus on results and disregard the relationship side of their work. So why do managers drive for results at the expense of relationships?

Unfortunately, as managers are promoted into higher levels in their organization, too many feel that they should become more dynamic and decisive. After all, they're in charge! And the more dynamic and decisive they become, the more likely they are to disregard maintaining and enhancing relationships while expediently focusing on their *drive for results*. After all, isn't that all that matters?

The fact is, the more relationship-conscious employees are, the quicker they become disenchanted with managers who rule with selfish expediency, pursuing individual and departmental goals that are *self*-focused without considering the rest of the team. Employees want to be respected and invited to use their minds instead of just blindly following orders. They can quickly become disenchanted with supervisors who express, "My way or the highway!" or "Do it because I said to!" or "Do it because I'm the boss!"

What happens next is predictable—and avoidable. The good employees quit because they feel undervalued. The mediocre employees stay because they're content with a paycheck and with being told what to do. The manager never changes, and when new employees are hired, it isn't long before the cycle begins again.

Betsy Brown Braun writes: "Prepare the child for the path, not the path for the child." All too often, this philosophy plays out backwards with well-meaning parents who believe their task is primarily to prepare the path for their children. These parents remove obstacles, smooth out the rough places, and generally make life a painless, trouble-free experience.

What happens on the inside (*how* the child is maturing) will have far more influence on the child's future life than the external things that tend to consume the parents' energy and emotions.

This also applies to the workplace. Most managers, while intelligent and well-meaning, tend to expediently "prepare the path" to drive for results. They "tell" their subordinates the results (the *what*) they want with little or no input (the *how*) from their subordinates.

Few managers realize how a relationship-oriented approach would prepare the employees for the twists and turns along the path as they serve customers, suppliers (yes, serve suppliers), and each other. Employees who feel valued are much more willing to go the extra mile when those twists and turns happen—and they always happen.

An employee's sense of ownership over a product or process translates into better customer service, better accuracy, a better attitude overall, and a more positive workplace, even under stress. Treat an employee like a robot, however, and watch production and satisfaction plummet. Instead of taking ownership and trying to solve problems, employees, feeling overwhelmed and disregarded, will shift blame and responsibilities to others.

Which do you want at your organization?

Me, too. It's no contest. And an occasional gut-check regarding important areas of leadership can be extremely helpful—being proactive always pays dividends in the workplace.

This is critical: *Every manager can become a more effective leader with some effort, a willingness to change, and acceptance of a big-picture view of his or her role within the organization.*

Below are four quick questions you can ask yourself to determine how you leverage this important area of enhancing *relationships* as you drive for *results*. Ask yourself, "How often do I . . ." and rate yourself accordingly from 1 to 5 (1 = never, 2 = almost never, 3 = sometimes, 4 = almost always, 5 = always).

How Often Do I . . .

Listen to others?

1 - 2 - 3 - 4 - 5

Communicate with coworkers and direct reports?

1 - 2 - 3 - 4 - 5

Understand, cooperate, and collaborate with others?

1 - 2 - 3 - 4 - 5

Praise and appreciate those around me?

1 - 2 - 3 - 4 - 5

If you really want to understand your scores in the above areas, ask a trusted friend to gather anonymous feedback on these questions from your coworkers, supervisors, and direct reports. You may find that your personal results vary from the results you receive from others. When you are able to accept them with an open mind, these results have the potential to transform your leadership! They did for me.

Pause for Reflection:

1. *How did you rate?*

2. *Did you learn something about yourself?*

3. *What steps can you take today to start earning the enthusiasm, initiative, and devotion of your employees?*

By Word and Deed

When employees work hard, they like to receive simple recognition for achievement of the results, even when it was a team effort. Self-centered managers go around spreading news of the results as though they were the only ones who accomplished it. Actions can speak even louder than words to signal, "I recognize how hard you are working" or "I care about you." Simple examples of thinking of others include going to the hospital to visit an ill employee or an employee's family member; initiating an invitation for an employee to take off early to care for a sick child at home; or sending birthday cards and employment-anniversary cards to employees. Look for opportunities to acknowledge and express concern for employees, and they will respond in kind.

Of course, this can be challenging, particularly with constant pressure to deliver results. In our modern, hectic business environment, it is easy to slip into fulfilling our own narrow needs—such as driving for results in pursuit of a promotion or pay raise—without giving sufficient attention to the needs of other employees and the overall needs of the organization and its customers. Even a manager who is bright, knowledgeable, dedicated, decisive, and dependable may be impatient and intolerant at times when dealing with others.

This happens when managers think they have to give up results to enhance relationships. But here's the good news: it is not an either-or scenario.

Effective Leaders Wear Two Hats

Regardless of title or job position, I have found that we all wear two hats. One is a leadership hat, and one is a management hat. People tend to wear one hat more than the other, and we call that a bent or bias toward either managing or leading. When you wear your leadership hat, your focus is on people (relationships). When you wear your management hat, your focus is more on things (results).

Despite my bent toward building relationships (leading), I discovered over the years that I also had a knack for getting things done. And it was *not* because I was good at obtaining results (managing) but because I surrounded myself with people who were great at getting results. I learned to surround myself with talented managers whose management skills far exceed mine in certain areas. They know how to follow through, implement, execute, and get results. Their skills and abilities serve to complement and complete my natural strengths. Remember: work smarter, not harder.

As our business grew, I often put on my relationship hat and had discussions about our people (e.g., recruiting). I would then put on my results hat and talk about business-related items (e.g., financial statements), and then I would switch back to my relationship hat to discuss people again (e.g., training our workers). I found that sometimes the best choice isn't one between two options; it's one that includes both options.

Best-selling author Jim Collins, in his book *Built to Last,* said, "Instead of being oppressed by the 'Tyranny of the OR,' highly visionary companies liberate themselves with the 'Genius of the AND.' . . . Instead of choosing between A OR B, they figure out a way to have both A AND B."

Collins went on to say that this was *not* about "balance," in which you go to the midpoint fifty-fifty or half and half. Instead, highly visionary companies have a tightly held ideology—their core values and purpose—that they preserve and never change *while* also stimulating vigorous adaptation and movement—accomplishing both at the same time, all the time!

We can apply this same principle as we learn to embrace both managing and leading. It is not about being a pretty good leader and a pretty good manager. It's about being an excellent leader *and* an excellent manager.

Drive for Results and Enhance Relationships

Effective leaders never lose sight of the fundamental importance of their need to oversee their team's drive for results. They need to be good at analyzing, planning, prioritizing, deciding, initiating, and following through. But they don't decide by themselves. And this is important. Rather, they make decisions in a participative way with their employees.

Fully effective leaders have learned that, as they drive for results, it is equally important to build, maintain, and enhance positive relationships. It's a matter of all teammates banding together with mutual respect, trust, understanding, and commitment to the organization's goals.

Leadership is not a function of titles; it is a function of relationships!

These leaders must be able to identify, select, coach, guide, support, and motivate people so they can achieve continual improvement. Perhaps most importantly, leaders must relate with employees in ways that will help them feel good about themselves, their work, and their organization.

You can achieve these key relationships by:

- Involving your people in the decision-making process.

- Keeping an open mind and respecting others' views.

- Encouraging communication, coordination, and cooperation among all your team members.

This focus on others is missing in the approaches of so many leaders. But you can see how we, as leaders, should see ourselves as servant-leaders. And the key to becoming the most effective *servant*-leader is to embrace both relationships and results (leading and managing).

So keep both your hats handy—you'll need them.

Before we continue to focus on the leader that you want to become, though, it's important to take a close, honest look at the type of leader—or manager—you are now.

Pause for Reflection:

1. *Do you find yourself wearing only one hat—the hat to drive for results?*

2. *Have you accepted the fact that you can learn how to improve and enhance relationships?*

3. *How can you "swap hats" today and further develop your leadership skills?*

Two Extremes to Avoid

My entire life, I have been asked to lead. Here is the interesting part—I never sought out a leadership role in anything.

When I was in high school, I was asked to lead in sports, the classroom, and a math club. In college, I was asked to take on leadership roles in my fraternity and in student government, including serving as student-body president. After taking over our small family business when my father unexpectedly died, I was asked to also take on leadership roles in a variety of nonprofit organizations, including my church and the Rotary Club, at both the local and international level. I was asked to serve on my national trade association's board of directors. The governor of Texas even asked me to run for the Texas State Senate, even though I was not active in politics.

I don't share all of this so you can pat me on the back. I share this as an example of the truth we have been discussing—that the key to becoming the most effective leader is to emphasize both relationships and results in your leadership. My understanding of this truth is, I believe, the reason others sought me out for leadership positions.

> Insight: The key to becoming the most effective leader is to emphasize BOTH relationships AND results in your leadership.

This type of leadership can be challenging, and it is not typically taught in business-school classes. When managing others without the necessary *knowledge* and *role models*, many people gravitate to one of these two extremes: the Taskmaster Manager or the Country Club Leader.

Most people's bent is to manage to achieve results, but sometimes a person with a results-based bent goes too far. They become a Taskmaster Manager. These managers have good intentions and tend to think that the drive for results is the solution to everything; they believe that enhancing relationships is too time-consuming and not as important as results.

On the other hand, some people's bent is to manage relationships. And when they go to the extreme, they become what I call Country Club Leaders. These leaders tend to be people pleasers. With good intentions, they spend an enormous amount of time visiting with people, loving on them, patting them on the back, and kissing babies. These people can be fun to be around, but very little gets done. They hope results will follow or expect that results will just somehow show up.

Which one would you choose to work for? When given those options, most people select the Country Club Leader because it sounds enticing, like a carrot dangled in front of you. However, I have observed most people will quit a Country Club Leader much sooner than a Taskmaster Manager.

Why? Because deep inside of us is a yearning to *accomplish* something worthwhile.

If I came home after working for the Country Club Leader and my wife asked me what I'd done that day, I would stutter and look confused because I would not be able to tell her what I'd accomplished. I'd probably respond, "I had fun at work, but I got little done for the day." It would not be too long before I would get tired of all the fun stuff and quit because of my desire to accomplish something.

On the flip side, if I came home after working for the Taskmaster Manager and my wife asked me what I'd done that day, I would proudly give her a long list of accomplishments. Even though I'd be tired and worn-out from work, I'd feel good about what I had achieved. However, I would only be able to withstand the "pressure cooker" for so long and would eventually quit.

The Effective Leader

Thankfully, there is a third option, and that is what I call the Effective Leader. For most people, it requires some changes and some work to get there, but leadership effectiveness is within your reach! In fact, *every manager or leader can experience exponential effectiveness by becoming an Effective Leader.*

Only a few people learn the skills to both build relationships (*how* they say and do) and get results (*what* they say and do)—in other words, leading *and* managing. This is the leader that employees long to work for, and when they find one, they usually make that job a career.

Pause for Reflection:

1. *Have others asked you to take on a leadership role not only at work but also outside your work life?*

2. *Which manager/leader above fits you? Which would you rather work for?*

We've turned our gaze inward to examine the type of leader you are now, we've considered different types of leadership and management, and we've explored the importance of valuing both relationships and results as you both lead and manage. Now we'll take another step along this journey to effective leadership: examining your leadership role models.

Role Models

Who are your role models? What have they taught you—or are still teaching you? One or two people will most likely come to mind. But if you put a little more thought into it, I bet you could make a list of eight to ten people who have shaped your life, either intentionally or inadvertently.

I have had a lot of people in my life, including my dad, who were positive role models for me. Once I started thinking about it, I was able to recall specific instances in my past—like snapshots of memories—that stood out as teachable moments.

My dad's best friend was like an uncle to me. When I was a kid, he let me drive the company van to make a furniture delivery out in the country—a stick shift, even—and I felt like the king of the world. After my father died, my wife and I could not afford two cars, so this man took me to work and brought me home every day for more than a year. He helped to position me for success in more ways than I can count.

In elementary school, my math teacher was a positive role model. He didn't simply instruct his students; he showed us that he cared deeply about us, and our lives, and he was willing to go the extra mile to help us learn. He was so encouraging to me.

Starting when I was a teenager, there were two men at my church who particularly influenced my life. They demonstrated strong and sound character, were men of integrity, and showed me through their actions and their words what it meant to live a life that reflected my beliefs.

In high school, there was a certain businessman who took an interest in me. Even though he had a successful home-building business, he also had a law degree, and he saw potential in me and encouraged me to attend law school. I was attempting to do so when my father suddenly died.

In college, there were a couple of professors and vice presidents who took me under their wing while I was student government president. One was the vice president of University Affairs, and the other was the vice president of Student Affairs. They showed me so much about how the university operated, and they recognized and nurtured my potential for leadership. After my father died, the vice president of University Affairs sponsored my membership in the Rotary Club, and the vice president of Student Affairs remained my friend for forty years.

When I took over running our small family business, a CPA, a banker, and a few businessmen helped me along the way. My dad had accounts at two different banks, and two bankers wanted us to shut down the business because of its debt load. However, one banker said to give me a chance, and the others finally agreed. That one banker is still a good friend of mine today. In Rotary Club, I met several businessmen who were always available to coach me on business issues, which was hugely helpful during that early period of running the business.

Then there was Jim Lundy, who served as my personal friend, coach, and mentor for over twenty years. Acting like a father to me after the passing of my own, this great man would drop just about anything to help me become a better leader and a better person. His recommendations never failed me. Jim helped me understand the value of focusing on relationships, and he was passionate—and I mean passionate—about good customer service. He taught me how to lead others and manage a business in a principled way for better results. Jim was the author of the best-seller *Lead, Follow, or Get Out of the Way,* and his client list was impressive, including such giants as IBM, General Mills, Hewlett-Packard, 3M, General Dynamics, and American Express. But I'll remember Jim for his friendship, advice, and example of how to lead and live.

All of these people poured into my life and changed my future for the better. Take the time to make your own list and reflect on the people who have made you who you are today. In the same spirit, what I aim to do now by writing this book is to mentor others and pass on what I have learned over the years. You can pass it on, too.

In fact, one way to strengthen your own leadership effectiveness is to emulate qualities or techniques you admire in other leaders who have touched your life, including the act of mentorship. If you've been given the gift of mentorship over the years, a simple way to honor the legacy of those who poured knowledge and time into your life is to do the same for others.

Another way is to intentionally embrace the shared characteristics of effective leaders. Evidence from extensive research done by best-selling author Jim Collins in his book *Good to Great* revealed that enduring, visionary companies were led by effective leaders that he called *Level 5 Executives*. These Level 5 Executives are great role models who have two paradoxical characteristics—personal humility and professional will.

Personal Humility

Contrary to the commonly held notions about top-performing leaders, Level 5 Executives are undeniably humble. These great role model executives:

- Had ambition for the company rather than for themselves.
- Set up their successor for even greater success.
- Displayed modesty and were never boastful.
- Acted with calm, quiet determination on principled standards without relying on charisma.
- Gave credit for the company's success to other people, external factors, and good luck.

Professional Will

Though humble, these leaders were marked by an intense professional will. These great role model executives:

- Were driven to produce sustainable results.
- Had unwavering resolve to do whatever needed to be done to make the company great, no matter how difficult.
- Settled for nothing less than the standards set to build a great company.
- Blamed themselves (*not* other people, external factors, or bad luck) when things went poorly and took full responsibility.

Only a few leaders ever become Level 5 Executives. Those who have done so became great role models. They have learned to integrate the ability to maintain and enhance relationships (*how* they say and do) with the drive for results (*what* they say and do).

They experience exponential effectiveness in their leadership—through other people, their effectiveness is multiplied, not merely added. They experience not only more results and success but also better results.

Pause for Reflection:

1. *Who are your leadership role models?*

2. *How have they had a positive impact on your life?*

In the next chapter, I will explain the exponential impact an effective leader has on an organization. And you will see for yourself the benefits of becoming this type of leader.

CHAPTER TWO:
The Fastest Way to Improve Your Leadership

LEVERAGE YOUR LEADERSHIP AS YOU
VALUE AND EMPOWER PEOPLE

"The ear of the leader must ring with the voices of the people."

WOODROW WILSON

Early in my career, I began searching for information to help me improve my leadership. I knew there was more to leading a company than just occupying the corner office and signing paychecks. Something was missing. In my quest for information and teaching on leadership, I purchased virtually every relevant book and resource I could find. However, each time I dug into a newly acquired book or product, something told me that it did not provide what I was seeking. Eventually, I came to realize that most of this information focused on how to manage *things* rather than how to lead *people*.

The breakthrough did not arrive until the late 1990s. While attending a John Maxwell conference on his new book, *The 21 Irrefutable Laws of Leadership*, I finally found the leadership material I had been looking for all those years. John's materials resonated so deeply with me because he boiled leadership down to simple, people-centric principles. They were easy to understand and to put into practice, and they made complete sense.

You see, John's teaching acknowledged that a leadership style of simply driving people toward the goal misses an important opportunity to *lead them* through building personal connections and relationships. As I began to develop my leadership, I discovered an important truth: every leader can experience exponential effectiveness by employing the two "R" factors—as you drive for *results*, also maintain and enhance *relationships*.

The Effectiveness Quotient

I coined this term to describe or rate a person's level of effectiveness. Imagine if you were to rate a person on a scale from 1 to 10 regarding his or her focus and drive as these qualities related to results. You would also rate the person from 1 to 10 on focus and intention as related to building and maintaining relationships. This person's effectiveness quotient would be the "results rating" times the "relationship rating." So a person with a results rating of six and a relationship rating of three would have an Effectiveness Quotient of eighteen.

As I mentioned, most managers have a *bent* or bias to drive for results (managing things). Concerning the Effectiveness Quotient graph below, I have found that it's not unusual for people to rate pretty well on results and fairly low on the relationships part of leadership.

Look at the lower-left rectangle on the graph on page 35. It represents the effectiveness of someone who reaches a six on the results scale (about average) and a one on the relationship scale (very low). This person would focus on the bottom line and the end results of his or her work. Also, it's fair to say that he or she probably doesn't care much about building and

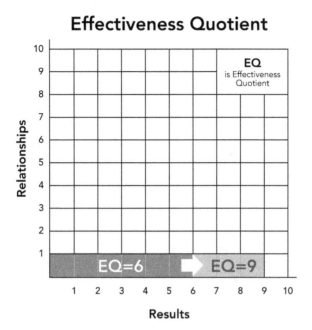

enhancing relationships. Yet even for those whose effectiveness is represented by the smallest shaded area on the graph, hope is not lost. They have some options to increase their level of effectiveness.

Focus on Results

The first option is to work diligently to increase the drive for more results and excellence. The goal would be to raise that six to a nine. If this person worked individually and drove others with great intensity to achieve this, his or her Effectiveness Quotient would have increased by only 50 percent, and there would probably be "dead bodies" lying around. There'd be better results, but at the expense of the majority of this person's relationships—both professional and personal.

Emphasize Relationships

The second option is for this person to strive to increase his or her people skills and level of relationships. You might be thinking, "Bobby, if I take time to focus on people and relationships in my business, won't my results suffer?" That's a good question! I have learned that it is not an either-or situation. Let's look at the second Effectiveness Quotient graph.

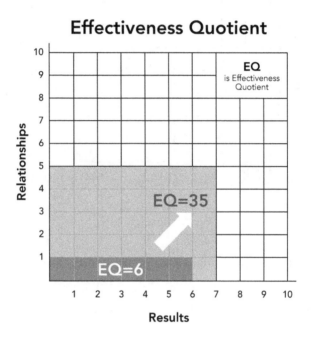

Suppose the leader now raises his or her relationship skills from one to five. In my experience and observations, the level of the leader's results will also increase, possibly from six to seven, with no added intentional effort in that area. The total Effectiveness Quotient will now be 35. The leader will have *exponentially* increased his or her original effectiveness of six by 583 percent simply by focusing on the relationship part of leadership.

Observation: When you increase your relationships, it has an exponential effect—your results increase as well.

The truth is that when leaders learn the skills to develop and emphasize both relationships *and* results, their effectiveness is multiplied, not just added. Even if it requires extra effort and time, even if it takes you out of your comfort zone, the results—the exponentially larger results—speak for themselves.

Pause for Reflection:

1. *What kind of books are you reading and what webinars are you attending? Are they about how to manage the things of your business? Or how to lead your people?*

We've seen how focusing on results and relationships can multiply your effectiveness, allowing you to achieve far superior outcomes in your organization. Next, we'll consider how you can begin to see truly amazing gains by multiplying not just your individual effectiveness but also the effectiveness of your whole team.

First, though, we have to consider why, for better or worse, the buck stops at the top.

Use Leadership Math to Multiply Your Team's Effectiveness

Have you ever noticed that when organizations are in trouble, they rapidly seek new leadership? We see it in large businesses, sports teams, and churches—the assumption that the subtraction of one person at the helm and the addition of a new person will equal instant growth.

How often have you seen a sports franchise try to turn things around by firing a head coach and hiring a replacement? Every time the NCAA Division I College Basketball Tournament starts, I wonder how many college basketball coaches will lose their jobs after March Madness fades away. Out with the old, and in with the new.

When a business is losing money, it hires a new CEO. When a church is stumbling, it searches for a new pastor. When our country is facing hard times, we elect a new president.

Insight: People understand that as the leader goes, so goes the organization.

In his book *The 21 Irrefutable Laws of Leadership,* John Maxwell tells us that we are the lids on our own success. I have found this to be true—my own leadership skills are often the lid, or limiting variable, on my personal life and business success.

If your leadership skills are strong, the organization's lid is high. But if your leadership is lacking, then the organization is limited. The obvious question then becomes, "What is the best way to develop my leadership?" The answer is to grow yourself. Greater leadership effectiveness is within your reach, and you can learn the skills needed. You only need to be willing to grow.

Your first job is to grow *you,* not your business.

There are two truths I want you to remember:

- *Your organization will always be defined by your leadership.*
- *The size of your business reflects the size of your leadership.*

Think about those two statements for a second. If you don't like your current results, you can change them. In fact, every person can increase the effectiveness of his or her team by leveraging the math of leadership.

Results by Addition

When you think like a manager, focusing on things and the drive for results (*what* you say and do), you'll see results by *addition*. If there are four "tens" and one "five" on a team with five individuals, the sum of their individual effectiveness scores is 10 + 10 + 10 +10 + 5 for a total of 45. If the fifth person grows from a five to a ten, the team's total effectiveness score rises to 50, an increase of 11 percent.

That's certainly not a bad gain. But watch what happens when you foster an environment of teamwork rather than individuality.

Results by Multiplication

When you think like a leader, focusing on people in order to maintain and enhance relationships (*how* you say and do) *and* also driving for results within that environment, you will see results by *multiplication*.

Look what happens to the group's impact when the multiplying effect of teamwork is considered. Through exceptional communication, coordination, and cooperation, the first team might be as effective as 10 x 10 x 10 x 10 x 5, having an effectiveness score of 50,000. But if the fifth person can grow from a five to a ten through his or her own commitment and the help of others, the team's effectiveness could grow a whopping 100 percent to an effectiveness score of 100,000! You get not only *more* results and success but also *better* results. Why? Because now you have a peak-performance team in which members communicate, coordinate, and cooperate among themselves and other departments and divisions. You see, when we consider team performance, the Effectiveness Quotient still applies. In fact, with teams, the "Enhancing Relationships" factor in the quotient becomes even more important! Once the team sees how valuable the synergy is, there is no limit to what they can accomplish by working together and helping each other reach goals.

Pause for Reflection:

1. *Do you want to lift your success lid?*

2. *Are you ready to grow YOU?*

3. *How can you use leadership math to multiply your effectiveness?*

By now, hopefully you see how the multiplying effects of teamwork can boost your organization. Before you can fully capitalize on team members' strengths, though, you must work to understand them. One key point is particularly important, and—believe it or not—although it's all about your team and who they are, it revolves around their leader. It revolves around you.

Do You Lead Followers or Leaders?

After leading my company for several years, I believed that I had the principles of leadership down. As I drove for results (*what* I said and did), I maintained and enhanced relationships (*how* I said and did).

Driving for Results:

- I had gotten better and better at the skills required to manage things for results.

- I had surrounded myself with some very good managers who were even better than I was at managing things for results.

Enhancing Relationships:

- Since this was my bent, it was easy for me to maintain and enhance relationships by being respectful and thoughtful of people.

- I had many of the attitudes of a servant-leader.

I had even served in leadership roles at several nonprofit organizations. There's one thing I learned for sure when serving in nonprofits:

Volunteers will test your leadership skills to the maximum.

Why? Because volunteers don't have to be there. They can jump ship anytime they wish. And when they drop the ball—and many do—you can't throw a temper tantrum.

There's another reason my nonprofit leadership roles were challenging: many of the people I led were also leaders. I was actually learning how to lead leaders, not just followers! I didn't know it at the time, but my experience in the nonprofit world helped prepare me for the next stage of leadership in my company.

It was about this time that I attended a business workshop taught by Dr. Jim Lundy. During the workshop, I had an epiphany that flat-out "floored me," as we say in West Texas. I learned that I was attracting and developing followers rather than leaders.

In 2013, I had the pleasure for one year of being part of a group of sixteen leaders who were mentored by John Maxwell. In one of the discussions, John stated, "Ninety percent of all leaders lead followers." For a very long time, I was a part of the 90 percent. You see, before that paradigm shift at Jim Lundy's workshop, my true motives were to:

- Hold on to the power instead of sharing the power.

- Take recognition for our success instead of sharing the recognition by reproducing myself in others.

- Spend time with people instead of investing time in them.

- Focus on correcting people's weaknesses instead of focusing on people's strengths.

The Key Component

I discovered the one key component that's necessary if you want to cultivate leaders and not merely direct followers: you must allow your employees to get involved in the decision-making process. As discussed in the last chapter, this serves to nurture the relationships needed for you to thrive as a leader and for your company to grow and prosper even as you execute better, more informed decisions. It has other benefits, though—it also allows your employees to grow, take ownership in decisions, and ultimately transition from followers to leaders themselves.

Although I had good intentions and thought I was helping our people, for years I kept the decision-making process as a responsibility I carried alone. This way of thinking may have been left over from the early days, when we were a much smaller family business and I did just about everything. Or perhaps it was my pride that caused me to think I was the only one who had the ability to go through the decision-making process. Or maybe it was a combination of both. But I believe that all leaders can experience extraordinary results by incorporating new key components into their leadership.

Enhancing relationships has two components: how you say things and how you do things. I failed in the doing. Once I began to encourage our people to be actively involved in the decision-making process, I was able to build a peak-performance team that achieved extraordinary results.

Do you lead followers or leaders? What are your motives? Your answers will determine the potential of your leadership!

Pause for Reflection:

1.   *Are you leading followers, or are you developing leaders around you?*

2.   *What are your true motives?*

3.   *Are you missing a key leadership component?*

You've now turned your gaze inward for several different areas: you've examined whether your natural bent is to be a leader or a manager, considered your ability to wear two hats and drive for both results and relationships, and reflected on whether your intentions are to lead followers or develop leaders.

At this point, you should already have a much clearer understanding of your current leadership style. To dive even deeper, here is the next question we must ask . . .

Do You Focus on Efficiency or Effectiveness?

At a recent family dinner, I posed a question for some fun discussion. I challenged everyone to come up with word pairs that are almost always said *together* and that have the word "and" between the two words. Everyone joined in, and I was surprised to see how many word pairs we came up with. It was amazing!

In the food category, we came up with word pairs such as "salt and pepper," "peanut butter and jelly," and "macaroni and cheese."

In the business and professional category, we came up with word pairs such as "policies and procedures," "roles and responsibilities," "cause and effect," "symptom and root cause," "efficient and effective," and "leading and managing."

As you can imagine, this game went on and on to the point that it became downright silly. Even after we got home, someone would occasionally yell out another word pair. Of course, I loved the family fun this encouraged. But I found it interesting that these word pairs typically appear in a certain order and are almost always said jointly, as though they need to work together for the best results. We all have a tendency to categorize and prioritize, to place concepts or items into a certain structure and order. With these word pairs, we often imagine the pair as a single item or as one item automatically following the other. Yet this is not always the case. Later that evening, I reflected on the word pairs we named in the business and professional category, particularly *efficiency* and *effectiveness*.

Every leader and manager can achieve greater success by viewing matters through the lens of efficiency and effectiveness. These represent two useful viewpoints, and while they sound similar, they mean different things. Having one does not automatically ensure the other will follow. They are also commonly misused and misinterpreted, so let's compare and contrast them here.

Leaders and Managers:

- People with a manager's mindset have a bent toward efficiency.
- People with a leader's mindset have a bent toward effectiveness.

The most successful organizations understand that they need both efficiency *and* effectiveness.

Survival and Success:

- Efficiency: Doing things right that determine your survival.
- Effectiveness: Doing the right thing that determines your success.

Efficiency Focuses On:

- Getting the maximum output with minimum resources.
- The process—the way of doing things.

Effectiveness Focuses On:

- Achieving the goal.
- The end result—the final outcome.

Regarding the Status Quo and Change:

Efficiency:

- Is concerned with maintaining the status quo.
- Keeps things orderly to be efficient and requires discipline and rigor.

Effectiveness:

- Believes in meeting the end goal by considering any variables that may change in the future.
- Keeps the long-term strategy in mind and is therefore more adaptable to the changing environment.

Repetition and Innovation:

Efficiency:

- Requires documentation and repetition of the same steps.
- Avoids mistakes and errors.

Effectiveness:

- Encourages people to innovate and discover different ways to achieve the desired goal.
- Is not afraid to make new mistakes.

If you were being efficient but *not* meeting the requirements of the organization's stakeholders (owners, investors, donors, customers, clients), efficiency would be of little use to anybody. In a similar way, effectiveness may result in success, but at what cost?

Insight: It is interesting that when you take or accept an extreme position, life gets out of balance, and it restricts your potential results.

So we must adapt ourselves as the occasion dictates by understanding that the most successful organizations need both efficiency (managing) *and* effectiveness (leading). This is why leadership is *not* better than management. It is a different function. And great leaders need great managers to maximize their potential.

So don't forget to view today through the complementary lens of efficiency and effectiveness. I guarantee it will improve your vision!

Pause for Reflection:

1. *What is your primary lens?*

2. *Are you restricting your potential by being stuck in an extreme position?*

3. *How can you improve your leadership/management vision?*

To switch metaphors, it's time now to take the different ingredients we've been trying and tasting to see what kind of dish will produce the most delicious results. We each have a winning recipe we can follow; it's time to discover yours.

The Secret Sauce for Success

As a young boy, Saturdays were my special days. Often, my dad would take me to lunch at a tiny downtown café where the specialty was chili dogs. I always had mine with cheese, onions, and extra mustard. To this day, those were the best chili dogs I have ever eaten.

The owner, a humble man with a heavy Greek accent and a gentle smile, would say hi to everyone coming in as he prepared the food and offer thanks when each customer left. As an adult, I continued the family tradition by bringing my boys to eat the best chili dogs in the world until the owner retired.

During weekdays in the café, you would find customers from all walks of life: men and women in business attire, "street people," and everyone in between. But the owner treated everyone with dignity and respect no matter their status in life.

One day, while I was eating one of those delicious chili dogs, I overheard a conversation between the owner and a customer: a businessman who owned multiple restaurants in town. The businessman was trying to pry out of the café owner the ingredients for his secret chili sauce by pounding him with question after question. The café owner just continued to smile and shake his head, signaling no while still treating the man with kindness and respect.

The chili dogs *were* phenomenal, but the businessman was missing the real reason for that café's success.

My Secret Sauce

There are a lot of reasons for my successful business, and over the years, I personally have received much credit for that success. But my success is really due to our people, the folks who "made the railroad run every day." That is my secret sauce—people, people, people!

So what makes a secret sauce, well, secret? The ingredients! And when it came to my business, I had two secret ingredients in my recipe for success: *what* I said and did along with *how* I said and did things.

Secret sauce ingredient #1 was *what* I said and did (as I drove for results). You can break this ingredient into two unique parts:

- *What* I said: Asking the right questions. What is the goal? Are we making progress?

- *What* I did: Working on the "things" of our business—strategies, tactics, performance goals, product and service offerings, policies and procedures, organization structure, operating practices, facilities, equipment, financial statements, and so on.

Secret sauce ingredient #2 was *how* I said and did things (by enhancing relationships). This ingredient also breaks down into two unique parts:

- *How* I said: *Saying* encouraging words to people, thanking them, and praising them.

- *How* I did: I combined this part of the recipe in two distinct ways that focused on the "people" in our business.

    1. *Doing* acts of kindness for people, patting them on the back, and shaking their hands (while I was thanking and praising them).

    2. *Doing* by consistently involving our people in the decision-making process. This proved to be the game-changing part of my secret sauce recipe! As we've seen, this is a key part of participative leadership.

For years, I thought I had these two ingredients down. Our company was growing, people enjoyed working there, and we were successfully profitable. However, it was not until I discovered how to combine the second part of *doing*—participative decision making—that we created a company in which people thrived and profits soared beyond my wildest dreams.

I believe these are truths that can help *any leader* create an award-winning secret sauce for his or her organization! Although it took me a while to discover these principles, I can help you implement these strategies in your own organization—and to do so much faster than I did by learning from the School of Hard Knocks.

I am dying to share with you the details that make a big difference in actually implementing these strategies, but first, I need to address some common problems and misconceptions that I have seen hold leaders back from making tremendous progress in this area. As an organization grows, the leader gets further and further away from the people on the front line, and two problems begin to crop up.

The First Problem

The first problem is that most leaders "don't know what they don't know." And they think they know all of the problems, challenges, and opportunities of their organization. This thinking is strongest among founders or leaders who have been in the organization for many years and who are bright and knowledgeable.

Also, they tend to think that their problems and frustrations (which are symptoms) stem from their employees—that is, until these leaders finally look in the mirror and recognize that they are the problem (the root cause). That is why John Maxwell said, "Everything rises and falls on leadership."

I have found that most leaders don't ask their employees to offer input for ideas to address the problems, challenges, and opportunities they are experiencing on the front lines. However, some of the current frustrations these leaders face come from lack of awareness of the real underlying problems in their organization.

Regardless of whether their businesses are just treading water or enjoying smooth sailing, little do they know that they just may be steering their "ships" right toward an iceberg. Like that fateful night with the *Titanic*, their lack of knowledge could wind up sinking the business.

The Iceberg of Ignorance

This principle is powerfully illustrated by the acclaimed study by consultant Sidney Yoshida known as "The Iceberg of Ignorance." As shown below, the study concluded: "Only 4% of an organization's front line problems are known by top management, 9% are known by middle management, 74% are known by supervisors, and 100% are known by front line employees."

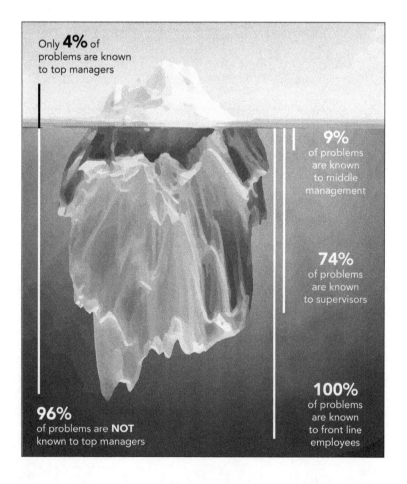

Only **4%** of problems are known to top managers

9% of problems are known to middle management

74% of problems are known to supervisors

96% of problems are **NOT** known to top managers

100% of problems are known to front line employees

Why are these findings important? Because if the problems, challenges, and opportunities remain unknown to leadership, this ignorance will impede the execution or diminish the results of even the best-laid plans.

The good news is that most leaders have a lifeline of valuable information and insights right under their noses—in their front-line employees. But most leaders don't notice this lifeline; they think that their own skills and expertise are good enough to navigate the waters of business.

The Second Problem

The second problem I have found is that some leaders think they *do* include their people as they make decisions but, in reality, don't truly involve their people in a meaningful way. These leaders ask (on a limited basis) their employees to offer input for ideas regarding the problems, challenges, and opportunities they are experiencing on the front lines. They might engage their people in conversation when they cross paths in the office and other work areas. They might even call folks, one at a time, into their office to solicit opinions and advice.

These leaders are, in fact, learning about some of the underlying problems in their organization as they go about talking to various individuals in the workplace. But they are missing the significant improvements that result from *group* discussion and brainstorming around the challenges and opportunities that exist and lie ahead.

The Best Solution: Participative Leadership

Have you ever noticed that when you read or hear something, you may learn interesting information or gain knowledge, but when you *experience* something, you gain understanding? As a leader, you can use the power of experience to build your team. One way is to include your people in meaningful discussions of today's challenges and opportunities! They're part of your team, so it just makes sense to include them and gain their support and feedback.

Effective leaders employ a participative style to focus on both relationships (*how* they say and do) and results (*what* they say and do).

The real question is not "Have you developed a team?" but rather . . .

Do you have individuals on a team or a TEAM of individuals?

These two options are worlds apart. You see the dramatic differences between them all the time in sports. In the first case, each player is primarily concerned with personal success, looking good, making the goal, and getting the spotlight—and the team suffers as a result. In the second situation, each teammate uses his or her abilities in service to a greater cause—the team's success—and, as a result, the team triumphs.

Individuals on a team win games, but *teams* of individuals win championships.

Over the course of time, most leaders will move in and out of several management styles as the need arises. There may be times when an authoritative style is needed, a style familiar to us from military operations—such as when troops are in battle, bullets are flying, and the ranking officer commands the troops to stand their ground. In a similar fashion, if there were a fire in your building, you would use an authoritative style to command your employees to leave the building. Although there are many types of management styles and specific situations may call for different approaches, I've learned that any leader can develop a championship team by adopting consistent use of the *participative* leadership style.

Participative leadership creates an open atmosphere where people's ideas and opinions are sought and respected. Participative-style leaders solicit input from employees at the very beginning of the decision-making process. But don't misunderstand; the participative leader is not asking employees to vote on matters affecting them or their departments. Instead, a participative-oriented leader seeks the benefit of employees' thoughts *before* he or she makes the final decision.

Years ago, several of our moving trucks began to show their age and required a large amount of maintenance. It was time to shop for replacement trucks. Instead of making an executive decision and informing the rest of the team after the fact, we pulled the drivers and crew members together to talk about buying new trucks. We asked them to do the research and spec out new equipment, which they readily agreed to do. During their research, they were shocked when they learned how expensive new trucks were. To my surprise, in an attempt to save money, they recommended that we leave out radios (this was before iPods and smartphones) and some other features. Since the drivers and crew members made those recommendations, their attitudes were very positive in spite of lacking features such as radios. Because they had been involved in the process and were given the opportunity to provide research and feedback, they felt a sense of ownership for these new vehicles.

Decisions like this are typically made by the CEO or a key leader. It makes sense that such a critical capital expenditure be the call of a top leader. Yet as our business grew, I saw how the participative leadership style deeply impacted the alignment and performance of our team. Ultimately, I made the final decision. But my decision making was informed by the research and recommendations of our team members. The end results were a good decision and a supportive and aligned team!

The Choice Is Yours

When challenges and opportunities arise, you have a choice to make. You can either stay with your normal decision-making process, or you can take a "risk" and tap the insights of your team. I believe you are actually taking more risk if you continue to make all the decisions without the help and input of your people.

When you are at the *beginning* of a decision-making process, you need all the input you can get to make the best, most informed decision. And your people, especially those who are on the front lines of your organization, hold the answers to many of your questions! Your people can bring front-and-center all the knowledge they possess regarding situations already present or approaching the organization to which the leadership is blind.

How do you get people involved? Empowering leaders are very intentional in the way they seek input from their employees. First, empowering leaders ask:

1. Who can help me make a better decision?

2. Who will have to carry it out?

3. Who will be impacted by it?

Secondly, the leader invites those employees (or an employee representing a group) indicated by the "Who" questions above to a group brainstorming session.

Thirdly, a facilitated group brainstorming session is conducted to generate ideas and thoughts about the topic at hand. During the session, it is important for the leader to ask questions and do a lot of listening.

By the way, this is not decision making by a committee. The leader still must make the final decision, but this simple process can equip him or her to make the best possible decision.

Three Key Benefits

Leaders who involve their people in this way of decision making will experience three key benefits. They'll make decisions that are better informed, their people will be more engaged with key decisions and their outcomes, and, finally, the organization will reach a level of team-initiated achievement that was impossible before implementing this process.

First, let's consider how your decisions will be better informed. When facing a decision, your individual insight will seldom be as broad and deep as that of your *team*. Your people are in a position to know what kinds of things might get in the way of implementing decisions that are made and plans that are laid out. Therefore, their input will grease the skids for implementation or execution of the decisions and plans.

As the leader, you have now afforded yourself more resources, ideas, and energy than you would have had on your own. You can devise better and more diverse alternatives when your team provides you multiple perspectives on how to reach your decision.

Next, consider ownership of ideas. When you sincerely solicit your employees' thoughts and ideas, they are more likely to see themselves as full-fledged members of an outstanding team, and they will be prepared to weather the impact of decisions and plans. As a team, they will share in the credit for victories and the blame for losses.

And if you implement this participative decision making (secret sauce ingredient #2), your employees are going to get excited about being asked for their ideas and involvement. They will also have a better understanding of and commitment to the decisions that they collaboratively set. They will be your biggest cheerleaders to champion the decision, and they will bring results far beyond your expectations.

What an excellent way for your people to feel a sense of achievement—and to earn the recognition for achievement—because they were involved in the development and implementation of decisions made.

Last, this approach leads to peak performance. Once I began to encourage our people to be actively involved and participate in the decision-making process, I was able to build a peak-performance *team* that achieved *extraordinary* results. I was able to maximize my team's potential and minimize their weakness when achieving results. And we did more as a team than we would have if I had made decisions alone. By contrast, if you lead like a lone ranger, your strengths and weaknesses are more exposed.

You too can achieve positive outcomes and extraordinary results by tapping this important principle—enhancing your relationships through participative decision making.

Pause for Reflection:

1. *What is in your secret sauce—your secret ingredients?*

2. *Have you struggled to get your people to support your decisions?*

3. *What might happen in your organization if you started to make decisions with the help of your team as described above?*

In the next chapter, we will take a look at the differences between *how* we work, communicate, and interact with people around us and *what* the final results of our work are—and why your approach to these two elements as a leader has the potential to sink your business or to raise it to new heights.

PART II
PROCESS AND CONTENT

CHAPTER THREE:
Embrace the *How* as You Pursue the *What*

TRANSFORM YOUR LEADERSHIP BY ADOPTING THE PRINCIPLE OF PROCESS AND CONTENT

"How you say or do something can make or break what you've said or done."

JIM LUNDY

John Maxwell says the greatest gap is the gap between knowing and doing.

In between, there is often an "aha" moment. Have you ever had one of these? A time when something finally made sense? Well, I had one the first time I experienced the effectiveness of what I call *process*.

I was rolling out a new mission statement at our company when it happened. My natural inclination at that time was to define the specifics and direction of an initiative, ask for some input from the team, and then go forward with rolling out my preconceived plan to the whole company.

This time, however, I took the time to really seek the perspectives and ideas of my employees. I changed my approach to *how* I accomplished the task at hand. I interacted with my team in a more open and intentional way. This was process-oriented focus.

And I was shocked by the response that I received through this new approach, which resulted in incredible buy-in from the team. We even developed a better mission statement!

Defining Process and Content

When we make decisions, outline plans, or convey instructions, there are two key factors involved. One is the *content* of what has to be decided. The other is the *process* whereby the decision is made. The content is the *what*—the results or end product of our efforts. The process defines the *how*—the way we interact with the people involved in the task.

Content

Technically, content is defined as "the amount of something in a container." Content is usually measurable and quantifiable. In the context of our life and work, when content is our main concern, we:

- Drive for results.

- Focus on things.

- Manage things.

- Concentrate on *what* we say and do.

In terms of leadership, one way to think of content is as the objectives we frame with and for those we lead. The content part of this principle is important. Without clear, well-communicated, meaningful, and attainable objectives, people are directionless. The people you lead need to know where you expect them to go!

To see an example of content, consider an organization's objective to develop a business plan to enter a new market. With content, the focus is on the final results of our work (the business plan), and the *what* is contained within the business plan.

Process

Process, on the other hand, is commonly defined as "a series of actions directed toward a specific aim." For our discussion, however, process is the essential "people" part of great leadership. Working well with others enables a leader to bring the very best out in his or her people. There are two important aspects to process:

- How we *say* things. The focus here is how we communicate and interact with people on a day-to-day basis. *How* we say something can significantly impact what the recipient of the message feels is being conveyed. Our body language and tone of voice can reinforce or contradict the message in the words we are saying.

- How we *do* things. This addresses how we interact with people to set and pursue our goals.

In our example of the business plan, the way we actually defined the business plan would be the process side of the task. Process deals with who has input on the objective and how we communicate with them. With process, the focus is on people—leading them, enhancing relationships, and intentionally monitoring how we say or do things.

The Principle That Can Transform Your Leadership

We need both process *and* content. The most enduring companies don't limit themselves to one solution or approach to a problem or challenge. Rather, they embrace two seemingly incompatible truths simultaneously.

Jim Lundy said, "How you say or do something can make or break what you've said or done." Process and content are often expressed using different words. Let's take another look at a list that matches expressions for process with corresponding expressions for content. We last saw it while examining the difference between Leading and Managing.

Process	Content
We enhance *relationships*.	We drive for *results*.
The focus is on *people*.	The focus is on *things*.
We lead *people*.	We manage *things*.
The focus is on *how* we say and do.	The focus is on *what* we say and do.

Although different words are used in different contexts, the concepts of process and content can be found in almost every aspect of business and even of life. Let's continue to look at our example of establishing a business plan. We can break this task down into two main areas.

The first area is the end result we would like to produce or accomplish. In this case, it is a business plan. This is the *what*, or the content piece of the task.

The second area focuses on the *how*, or process. This involves planning *how* we would involve *people* in preparing the plan and *how* we would communicate the finished plan to others.

If you're like most people, you tend toward content, not process. You like to focus on the task at hand, make decisions, delegate the supporting tasks, and "get 'er done"! But we have to focus on both. If you don't take time to work on your communication on the process side, you'll spend a whole lot more time down the road trying to repair the damage done by barking expedient commands.

Now, back to the gap that John Maxwell referred to. Our challenge as leaders is to decrease the gap between what we *know* and what we *do*. How can we apply what we have learned?

If you start to look for it, you'll see the potential to use this powerful duo of process and content in every area of your life. This concept literally transformed my leadership ability once I began to learn and apply its truths. These universal truths can transform your leadership ability, too, if you take steps to apply them in your life and business!

Pause for Reflection:

1. *Do you naturally focus more on content or process?*
2. *Can you break down one of your current projects into the two categories of process and content?*

The Leadership Paradox

As a leader, do you think you have time in your schedule to ask for input and decision-making help from your employees? Most leaders sincerely believe it takes too much time and effort to adopt a more participative, process-oriented leadership style.

This approach is too difficult to understand, they think, and they say to themselves, "I've got work to do, and my people need to be working.

Besides, I pay my people top dollar, and they don't need to be sitting around talking."

This type of thinking results in millions of employees throughout America who are:

- Unaware of the company's purpose statement (if there is one).

- Unaware of what the organization's goals are.

- Unclear about what is expected of them.

- Uncertain about others' perceptions as to how well they've been doing.

- Unsure about how they might be more effective or efficient.

- Uninformed about what degrees of freedom they have to pursue improvements.

Consequently, many potentially wonderful employees become frustrated and would likely agree with Jim Lundy's perceptive summary of this type of leadership in *The Employees' Lament:*

> "We, the uninformed
>
> working for the inaccessible,
>
> are doing the impossible
>
> for the ungrateful!"

That's the bad news. The good news is that these challenges represent unequaled opportunities for improved understanding. And the more open the communication atmosphere is for conversations vertically and horizontally, the greater the opportunity for people to address decisions in principled (instead of expedient) ways.

The paradox of process and participative leadership is this: what we bemoan as "extra and unnecessary" time invested in such an approach actually opens the door to achieving the results we have pursued for so long.

We need a focus on both process and content—not simply one or the other. If we can get past the scarcity mindset that leads to expedient leadership, we can enjoy the abundance that results from selfless leadership. Every participative-oriented leader can achieve positive outcomes and results as he or she taps the power of process and content!

Here's a list of some of the benefits:

- Employees feel good about themselves because they have a sense of achievement and enjoy receiving recognition for whatever has been achieved.

- Employees really appreciate being appreciated! They feel useful, and they welcome the opportunity to participate in any decision relating to their operations. They enjoy being respected as useful professionals whose opinions are important. They are excited to be respected as valuable "thinkers" as well as "doers."

- Customers appreciate being dealt with respectfully and are delighted because delighted employees enthusiastically serve them!

- Employees become truly inspired and enhance the organization's chances for success by virtue of their input.

- Morale and teamwork increase, which leads to improved performance and optimum results. The leaders' impact is multiplied, not just added.

- Because employees are involved in the decision-making process, there is buy-in and ownership. Through their early participation, people gain informal pretraining (knowledge and insights) that helps them effectively implement the decision. It's no wonder such folks become cheerleaders of the decision.

- Employees who are invited to engage in the process are likely to gain a better understanding of the results they are expected to achieve and why it is important to achieve these results.

- Employees who are part of the process feel their opinion is valued and are more likely to be committed to working within the team to achieve the results.

- Employees come to work on time daily, have a good attendance record, work for a higher purpose, and give a full day's work for their pay.

- As all of these factors come together, organizations experience both highly motivated employees and high-performance teams.

Clarence Francis said, "You can buy someone's time, you can buy someone's physical presence at a given place, you can even buy a measured number of skilled muscular motions per hour or day. But you cannot buy enthusiasm; you cannot buy initiative; you cannot buy loyalty; you cannot buy devotion of hearts, minds and souls. You have to earn these things."

Engaged employees are enthusiastic about their work, show initiative, and loyally devote themselves to further the organization's reputation and interest. This extra level of effort and contribution is called "discretionary effort." In business, this is like finding the goose that lays the golden eggs. How can you earn such discretionary effort from your team? By adopting the principles of process and content. It will take some extra time and effort, but the results will far exceed the additional investment in yourself and others!

Pause for Reflection:

1. *The best way to reach your goals may not be a straight line! Will you try this approach to leading and experience the Leadership Paradox?*

2. *What steps can you take today to start earning the enthusiasm, initiative, and devotion of your employees?*

Process, Content, and Relationships

In October of 1989, I attended a three-day workshop called TRAC 5000 led by Jim Lundy. During the workshop, Jim introduced the ideas of process as well as content. Although I didn't fully understand his teaching during the workshop, Jim was introducing me to the concept that *relationships are key to effective leadership.*

My first action step from the workshop was to create a mission statement for our company. A few weeks later, I called a company-wide meeting to introduce our mission statement. During the meeting, I explained to our people the meaning behind the statement and asked if they had any questions or suggestions to improve it. Since there were few questions and little discussion, I figured they understood and were in agreement with the mission statement. Next, I set out to find a printing company to design the layout and print copies to distribute throughout our company.

A few days later, Jim, my personal friend and a long-time mentor, stopped by my office to see how I was doing on my action steps from the workshop. I shared with great excitement that I had completed my first one. I showed Jim the mission statement that I'd created, explained how I had called a company-wide meeting to introduce it, how I'd shared the meaning behind it with our employees, and how, since there had been few questions and little discussion, I was going to have copies printed for everyone.

Jim was excited as well. However, he suggested that, before going to the printer, I go back to our people one more time for any questions or suggestions to improve the mission statement. I was surprised by his suggestion. I had already met with everyone, and it seemed too costly to bring everyone together again. He said he understood, but again suggested going back to our team one more time. He had one of those "just trust me" looks on his face. So I did.

A few days later, we scheduled another company-wide meeting for our people to look over the mission statement so they could ask questions and make suggestions for improvements. During this second meeting, questions and suggestions all of a sudden came out of the woodwork. People really got engaged and had some very good suggestions. I walked out of the meeting feeling that everyone—and I mean everyone—truly understood our mission statement.

In fact, since the second meeting went so well, I called a third company-wide meeting after making the suggested changes to show them to the employees. There was *even more* discussion for understanding, and a few more good suggestions were made. It was amazing how excited our people were over this. And I was excited to see everyone so engaged with the process. This was the first time that I could say every employee company-wide was of one voice and on the same page. At that meeting, I finally understood the concept of process *and* content.

At first, I was only focusing on the content (the results of having a mission statement so I could check it off my list of action steps). But Jim helped me understand the importance of good process (enhancing relationships between me and our people and also between each of our people). By encouraging our people to be actively involved in the decision, we built a peak performance team that achieved the results we desired.

And if you want to build a team that moves forward together toward your goals, understanding and implementing the concept of process *and* content is a great start.

Pause for Reflection:

1. *Why do you think we tend to overestimate the value of the content (the results we want to accomplish) and underestimate the value of the process (the relationships we need to enhance to build a team)?*

2. *Can you identify one way that you can tap the power of process with your team today?*

Process and Content Applies to Parents (and Leaders)

I recently spoke with a good friend who grew up in a very wealthy family, one so affluent that the children were driven to school by a chauffeur. This friend said, "If your dad gave you everything but never had time for you, the things would not mean anything because there would be no relationship attached to the things." What a powerful statement.

In this scenario, do you see how my friend's dad was focused on the things (the content) but not the relationship? I can almost hear him say, "I give my kids everything they could ever want." Yet the kids felt unloved and unappreciated and were desperate to spend quality time with their father. In the father's mind, the gifts proved that he loved his kids. But in his kids' minds, the effectiveness of his gifts was dependent on the depth of the relationship he had with his children. This represents the process part of the story, which speaks to the power of emotionally connecting with people to form strong relationships.

To be good parents, leaders, employees, and spouses, we actually need both process *and* content. We need both the "how" and the "what"—it is not one or the other. So for now, I want to continue to focus on *how* we do things—how we interact with people to set and pursue our goals. Because, as you'll find, how we do things matters.

Lessons from the Top

I enjoy learning about other leaders and observing what makes them successful. I've learned a lot from one chief executive whose greatest skill is perhaps the way he interacts with others. He achieved an incredible increase in corporate performance by changing the authoritative corporate culture to one best characterized as process-oriented teamwork. And it was not easy.

For thirty years, his organization had been run by the creative founder (a real genius), who made all the decisions himself and then dictated operating instructions to his three submissive—but frustrated—lieutenants. After the founder moved on, this chief executive took over. He began leading his team by seeking input from key employees before making major policy and strategy decisions. With this new approach, the company, which had grown 5 to 10 percent a year for thirty years, exploded with record-setting growth. During the next four years, he led the company to volume increases of more than 400 percent and profits that rose over 1,800 percent.

There's a lesson here for all of us!

Yes, it's awfully easy in the short run to make quick decisions on our own and to be curt and directive in giving instructions. (Just think about how much easier it might sometimes seem to pick up your child's room rather than to patiently give little Emily repeated instructions and direction.) However, at least in the workplace, it takes incredibly little additional time and effort to allow others:

- To contribute their thoughts on pending decisions.

- To encourage involvement.

- To ask for commitments instead of demanding them.

- To be constructive and supportive when seeking improvement.

- To be able to disagree without being disagreeable.

- To capitalize on the creative ideas and support of all those who can contribute to making good things happen.

What does it take to improve the way one interacts with others? An understanding of people's desires and needs, coupled with nominal investments of time and effort to tap the power of process, will yield wonderful long-term returns. I can confidently say from experience that the increases in morale and teamwork will lead to improved performance and results.

> *Pause for Reflection:*
>
> 1. *Are you failing as a leader? Perhaps the solution involves focusing more on your relationships with your team members.*
>
> 2. *Do you focus on what you do, how you do things with your team members, or both?*

Leverage Your Leadership

Let's return for a moment to the approach of developing leaders rather than followers, viewing it through the lens of process and content. Recently, I heard John Maxwell say, "You have two choices as a leader. You can lead followers, or you can develop leaders. And 90 percent of all leaders lead followers." What he was saying is that a lot of leaders are content just to have followers because developing leaders is very challenging and requires leading with a higher degree of focus and intention.

Leading leaders is difficult, and developing leaders is even more difficult. But if you can lead and develop leaders, your potential is unlimited. In John's book *Developing the Leaders Around You*, he writes that the leader's highest return is forming a dream team of leaders. Why?

1. Developing yourself as a leader gives you a good return.

2. Developing others as leaders gives you a better return.

3. Developing a team of leaders gives you a greater return.

Over the years, I have observed that leaders who lead followers are loyal to the company and dedicated to their job. They typically work twelve to fourteen hours a day.

However, I have also observed that leaders who lead followers are generally more focused on results (content: *what* they want to do). Their focus is not on relationships (process: *how* they do things) or on developing leaders.

Since we need both process and content, most of us will need to focus on how we interact with people to set and pursue our goals.

How Do You Lead?

Focusing on good process as well as content is a matter of style. Authoritarian managers are task-oriented and prone to rely on their position of authority when directing their employees. They leave little or no room for their employees to contribute to the decision-making process. In the extreme, these managers expect employees to follow orders without ever challenging them or questioning their command.

By contrast, participative leaders create an open atmosphere. They solicit input from employees at the very beginning of the decision-making process. But don't misunderstand; they are not asking employees to vote on the ideas or options discussed and arrive at a "group decision." Instead, participative leaders want the benefit of employees' thoughts before making a decision.

I have further observed that leaders who lead followers generally have an authoritarian style. They tend to focus only on the results and what they want to do. Leaders who develop leaders have a participative style. They tend to understand they need both relationships and results. Why? The more time you spend developing a stronger leadership team, the more your team will want to participate in the direction of the organization.

When you understand and implement the two-pronged approach of process and content, you'll multiply your impact as a leader.

Pause for Reflection:

1. *Are you leading followers, or are you developing leaders around you?*

2. *How would your team members describe your leadership style—more authoritarian or more participative?*

3. *Would it bring more clarity to your situation if you gathered your team members' opinions about your leadership style through an anonymous poll?*

Process, Content, and Making Decisions

As leaders, we make decisions every day. In some ways, you can boil leadership down to a series of decisions—some good and others bad. For years, I've made decisions in a particular way that leverages the power of process-based leadership. And I have used the term "process" to describe *how* we interact with people to set and pursue our goals.

In short, decisions create opportunities to lead. And anyone can increase his or her effectiveness as a leader by following this simple plan for decision making.

We have already examined how the participative leadership style can be employed when you have a large decision to make. As advised in chapter 1, you should gather an appropriate team to discuss the challenge or opportunity and resolve how it can most effectively and efficiently be addressed. Also, it's important to resist the temptation to start finalizing your own solutions before the meeting. To assemble the right people to include in this process, ask yourself three key questions: Who can help me make a better decision? Who is going to have to carry it out? Who will be impacted by it? This is part of the drive for relationships, and it produces phenomenal results.

Now let's go deeper into this process and apply the lens of process and content.

Time Well Spent

I've found that this approach usually involves engaging your team over a period of time through a series of meetings. A good four-step meeting approach looks like this:

1. Start with a meeting to expose your team to an idea, and then give them some time to let the idea sink in and "incubate."

2. Pull them together, and ask for and record their input and ideas.

3. Get them together again to review the plan, help "tweak" it, and reinforce "buy-in" from all concerned.

4. Have them review the final plan or solution just to see if there are any more ideas for changes or improvements.

This might sound like it will take more time and effort than simply giving orders (autocratic) or telling someone else to figure things out (delegative). So why would you want to adopt this procedure for your decision making?

First, it's based in a fundamental regard and respect for people.

Second, it usually produces better results than merely giving orders or shoving things off onto someone else.

Consider this example. Let's say a leader announces a new goal or product/service offering. All leaders must first focus on content (*what* they want to say and do). After the new goal or offering is announced, leaders have a choice. They must decide how much they want to invest in process (*how* they say and do—including how they involve people in decision making).

Content-oriented managers are focused on reaching the end goal and how to reach it most *efficiently*. They focus very little on process (*how* they interact and involve people). These managers devote much energy and time during the implementation phase. This extra effort is required in order to convince the team to get on board with an implementation plan that they had very little to do with forming.

The process-oriented leader is focused on achieving the desired goal as *effectively* as possible. These leaders realize that the relationships built and fostered among the team make a huge impact on the ultimate outcomes. They focus on *how* they say and do things as they press toward the goal. They spend more time up front with their team, soliciting opinions, brainstorming, and asking questions. They do spend more time focused on process, but they enjoy a smoother and shorter implementation phase due to the high level of ownership and engagement that results from this type of approach.

Content-oriented manager approach

| Content | Process | Implementation | ➡ | Results |

Process-oriented leader approach

| Content | Process | Implementation | ➡ | Results |

The results of these two approaches reveal a compelling truth: the up-front time invested in process-oriented leadership yields notably better results. The content-oriented approach might show results sooner than the process-oriented approach; however, any early advances of a content-focused approach will be eclipsed by a high-performing, unified team led by a process-oriented leader. And in some cases, the content-focused approach will produce *negative* results because of poor implementation.

I have learned that focusing on good process is the best way to obtain the desired result, and I have grown to absolutely trust a "process-oriented" approach to leadership. Why? Because when I trust good process, I always get good results—plus all the other benefits of people being involved in the process, such as buy-in and ownership by people who become cheerleaders of the decision.

Pause for Reflection:

1. *How do you make decisions?*
2. *Would you consider trying this approach to decision making?*

Process-Oriented Communication

Just as a process-oriented approach to decision making can radically boost your results and team cohesion, this same approach can work wonders in your communication skills. Anyone can improve his or her leadership by understanding the following truth: *how* something is said is often more important than *what* is said! When it comes to leadership, communication matters!

How do you communicate and interact with people on a day-to-day basis? If you haven't given that much thought, I challenge you to pay close attention to your conversations today. How you say something can significantly impact what the recipient of the message *feels* is being conveyed. Our physical actions and tone of voice can reinforce or contradict the message in the words we are saying.

When the way that something is said (process) conveys a different meaning than the actual words (content), the interpretation triggered by the process will prevail. For example, when two old friends meet after many years of separation, one might say, "George, you old dog!" The words themselves may be negative, but if they are spoken with a ring in the voice and a smile, George will have no doubt that his friend is delighted to see him.

The way things are said often overrides the meanings of the words themselves with sarcastic comments as well. A negative pitch of voice has the power to dominate positive words.

Leadership Communication Truth: If the way we say something is out of alignment with what we are saying, the way we say it will always dominate the communication.

Your English teacher always said that punctuation was important. And, as with punctuation, just changing what you say by using a pause (an auditory comma) can make a big difference in meaning, too. For example:

- Let's eat grandma!

- Let's eat, grandma!

See the difference? One sentence is quite disturbing, while the other is a simple call to dinner! But what about those who argue that content is all-important? "I may not have time to worry about how I say something," the content-oriented leader points out. "It's much faster to be brief and concise and get on with the work at hand. What's right is right, and that's all that should matter!"

To that point, I respectfully disagree. Yes, there are times when you can't worry about how you say something (although it might be better if you did!). But the majority of your communications should be well-thought-out, and whenever possible, you should consider how your message will be received.

When trying to build and strengthen interpersonal relationships, an attitude of "what's right is right" can be absolutely wrong! We may make no better investment than the small amount of time and effort required to improve the way things are said and done. Certainly, some conditions require quick, authoritarian action. However, during noncritical periods—which comprise the majority of the time in daily business life—the best leaders usually interact in a participative way.

Pause for Reflection:

1. *If the content is what is said, and the process is how we say it, where do you see the most opportunity for improvement in your leadership?*

> 2. *Have you ever had how you communicated (process) override what you were saying (content)?*
>
> 3. *How could you apply this truth at home as well as work?*

Why Don't People Focus on Process?

I've found that most folks tend to live their lives focused on things, not people. You know what I'm talking about—things like phone calls to make, materials or equipment to purchase, reports to complete, and financial statements to review. The more these things stack up, the quicker we want to handle them so we can get on with other things. These are the *what* items that we habitually focus on while often not slowing down long enough to adequately think about considerations regarding the *how*, or process.

So why don't people pursue process as well as content? Here is the problem: in our busy environment, we tend to expediently pursue individual and departmental goals that are self-focused. It is very easy to slip into expediently fulfilling *our own* narrow needs without giving sufficient attention to the *needs of others* and how we might better fulfill the overall needs of the organization and its customers.

It's natural for sales people to want to increase their sales. Similarly, manufacturing people want to reduce their costs, minimize the production of imperfect products, and eliminate lost-time accidents. Administrative people such as accountants and human resource staff members want to produce accurate records and minimize employee turnover, respectively.

In each of these pursuits, our focus tends to be on quickly and successfully handling the content targets of our own specialties without giving sufficient attention to *how* our challenges and opportunities fit into the organization's goals. Self-serving efforts to save a dollar might have two dollars' worth of negative consequences on another department.

In other words, practicing, "Ready, aim, fire!" should take precedence over, "Fire, ready, aim!" Expedient, departmental-focused achievements can give quick results, but they may also produce a feeling of personal satisfaction at the expense of big-picture team effectiveness.

Many Leaders Make Incorrect Assumptions

The following are some other reasons why people don't pursue process as well as content:

- A person who is bright, knowledgeable, dedicated, decisive, and dependable may also be impatient and intolerant when dealing with others.

- A leader may think he has to give up content to have more process. (As we've seen, this way of thinking is not correct. It is *not* either-or. To be the most effective leader requires embracing both process *and* content.)

- Some would question whether participative leadership means running your organization as a democracy. (The answer is no. As the leader, you always have ultimate authority and responsibility for decisions and results.)

- Some would even think that participative leadership means creating consensus decisions among all members of your team. (This assumption is likewise incorrect. Consensus decisions usually take forever to reach and yield diluted results.)

- Some also think that participative leadership is not always the right approach. (There may be times a process-oriented strategy isn't best, but it's generally the most powerful approach a leader can take when driving for results.)

There are many concerns that get in the way of leaders fully applying this principle of process and content. Anyone can, however, make conscious decisions to learn and leverage this powerful principle.

Pause for Reflection:

1. *Are you daily caught up in the routine and details of your life and business?*

2. *What can you do to change how you say and do things to become the most effective leader?*

Performance and a Paradox

Many of the great pioneers who came to our country and expanded our frontiers were seeking an environment in which they could have a greater sense of control over their own decisions. They were fed up with the dominating leadership of dictators and royalty. These rulers made unilateral decisions and dictated the goals to be pursued. When taxation without representation became sufficiently frustrating, our forefathers even risked their lives in the American Revolution. Our predecessors didn't like performing for apparently arbitrary authority figures then, and we don't like it now!

When we relegate people to carrying out someone else's orders, we prevent them from having a full measure of opportunity to achieve. They typically choose fight, flight, or submission in response.

Peak Performance

Peak-performance teams and organizations have clear, stretching goals and a can-do atmosphere. They employ people who have a high sense of urgency, the skill to implement plan-oriented action, and the ability to achieve dependable results. People won't get truly inspired to achieve peak performance unless they are asked for their input on what goals and processes are most:

- Challenging.

- Worthy.

- Achievable.

Market-based economies have repeatedly outperformed socialistic and communistic economies that are based on centralized, autocratic decision making. Similarly, on Wall Street and Main Street, we see organizations led by empowering leaders that reach performance levels that far exceed those of their peers.

So what happens when people *don't* pursue process along with content?

The Participatory Paradox

Unfortunately, as leaders are promoted into higher levels in their organizations, too many executives feel that they should become more decisive. After all, they're in charge! And the more bold and decisive they become, the more likely they are to disregard good process and expediently focus on content matters. Their singular focus on *things* becomes a trap that hinders their team's effectiveness and ultimately limits their overall results.

Employees want to be respected and invited to use their minds as well as to simply follow orders. They can quickly become disenchanted with supervisors who make decisions unilaterally or expect to be obeyed simply because they are the boss. This understanding affirms the well-known adage, "People don't leave companies, they leave supervisors!"

When we have problems communicating or interacting, we tend to blame the environment or someone else rather than ourselves. How easy it is to settle for an attitude such as: *I wish the other departments in our company would be more communicative and cooperative with us.* Or: *I wish others would listen to me.* Our content-focused approach becomes a trap that stifles relationships, limits results, and sabotages our best-intended efforts.

The Solution

Instead of first blaming someone else for strained relationships or substandard results, we should take a look in the mirror. Remember the self-evaluation you did in chapter 1? We should ask ourselves: How well do I . . .

- Listen to others?
- Communicate with coworkers and direct reports?
- Understand, cooperate, and collaborate with others?
- Praise and appreciate those around me?

How can we cultivate peak performance in order to maximize our success? The answer is simple but eludes most leaders. We obtain optimum results through participative decision making and leadership.

And therein lies the paradox. Most people assume that strong leadership means independent action and that the more total one's control is, the greater the results can be. Ironically, the reverse is true: the more you include others in decision making, the stronger your results and leadership. Likewise, the more you exert absolute control as a leader, the weaker your results and leadership will be.

Always remember that the most important things in the world aren't *things*. They're people and relationships! The pioneers and founding fathers understood this. Hopefully each of us will, too.

Pause for Reflection:

1. *Has a primarily content-focused approach trapped you into strained relationships and disappointing results?*

2. *Based on your calendar and daily agenda, which do you value more—people or things?*

Upping Your Leadership Game

As we wrap up this chapter, let's look at a couple of areas to which you can apply the principles we have been discussing and start to "up your game" in leadership.

Interviews

Interviewing prospective employees is the first key area where you can start developing your sensitivity to process. When you interview your next candidate, keep in mind the two important areas of process *and* content:

- The résumé tells us about *what* (content) a candidate has done.

- Ask questions to explore *why* (a process question) various things have been undertaken and *how* (a process question) the candidate's decisions have evolved. In this way, you can more accurately predict how the candidate will act and interact with other employees.

Goal Setting

A second key area to focus on in process-focused leadership is goal setting. Since success has been defined as the achievement of one or more predetermined goals, goal delineation is a great place to grow our leadership.

Those who strive to build peak-performance teams learn (often in the expensive School of Hard Knocks) that *how* goals are determined is *at least* as important as the substance of the goals themselves (*what* the goals are).

When I am asked whether an organization's planning and goal development should flow from the top down or from the bottom up, my answer is "Yes!" I'm convinced that these important tasks should be based on *dialogues, not monologues.*

Interviews and goal setting are two key areas where you can begin implementing your new focus on process, and I believe you will see great improvements. Then, as you continue to refine this approach, you will find opportunities everywhere you look—in your business and in all other areas of your life.

Pause for Reflection:

1. *Do you seek to understand the "why" and "how" behind a prospective employee's résumé?*

2. *In what ways can you include more of your team when you set goals for the coming quarter or year?*

The Results

A completely different atmosphere exists with a process-sensitive leader who respects his or her subordinates and who has the good sense to seek and appreciate input from employees! With participative decision making, employees can enjoy being respected for sharing their ideas. They can not only become truly inspired but also enhance the organization's chances for success by virtue of their input.

With your new focus on process, you are in a prime position to take your organization to the next level by adding another principle to your daily approach to leadership. For this next principle, you will need to consider more deeply the context, motivations, and consequences of your behavior and decisions—which is the subject of the next chapter.

PART III
PRINCIPLE VS. EXPEDIENCY

CHAPTER FOUR:
Direction Trumps Speed

DIRECT YOUR LEADERSHIP BY EMPLOYING A PRINCIPLED APPROACH TO BUSINESS AND LIFE

"Where principle is involved, be deaf to expediency."

JAMES WEBB

W hen our three sons were in high school, I would say to them, "When you get in the car with your buddies on Friday night, you already know how the night is going to turn out." They knew what type of activities their friends might be involved in, and they knew the choices they would be faced with. So I wanted them to decide *before* they were asked about going out on the town Friday night whether they were going to accept or not.

And if they chose to get in that car, I wanted them to decide *beforehand* how they were going to react to the *emotional* situations that would occur that night.

Your unchecked emotions will always override your intellect.

The consequences of an emotional, expedient decision impact your life like the heated water in the classic story of how to boil a frog. The premise is that if a frog is placed in boiling water, it will jump out. But if it is placed in cool and pleasant water that is gradually heated, it will not perceive the danger until it is too late and will be cooked to death.

The same principle applies to people. If we make decisions based on what "feels good at the moment" and simply "go with the flow," we will often wind up in hot water! The expedient decision to take the easy route will lead us into situations where we'll suffer negative consequences for our actions (or lack thereof).

But if we make principled decisions based on what we know to be true and right, we'll experience less "self-made trouble" and greater success!

When you evaluate your behavior based on these two categories, you'll discover that virtually every action or decision you make can be described as either principled or expedient.

Expedient Behavior

People who behave *expediently* do what's easiest and quickest or what makes them the happiest in the *short run*. They tend to make emotional decisions that are reactive in nature. Deep down, expedient behavior is most often rooted in *fear*. Such behavior eventually leads to undesirable results and negative consequences—even addiction or death.

Principled Behavior

However, a person who exhibits *principled* behavior believes that today's short-term pain, sacrifice, and investment of time, energy, and money will eventually bring long-term growth, blessings, and success.

Principled behavior is rooted in *faith*. Principled behavior aligns you with time-tested ways to methodically create a successful life.

In the following sections, we'll explore and clarify the important differences between these two approaches. By the end of this chapter, you'll understand the painful pitfalls of emotion-driven expedient behavior and the immense benefits to character-driven principled behavior.

Pause for Reflection:

1. *Have you experienced the "boiling frog effect" in your own life?*

2. *Are you more principled or more expedient in your behavior?*

The Unexpected Outcomes of Expediency

Have you ever made a bad decision? I have made many, but one stands out in my mind because it was a public decision. I've thought quite a bit about what went wrong. Although it wasn't obvious at first, I have discovered the root cause, which is present in many of our bad decisions.

In 1988, the governor of Texas asked me to run for the Texas State Senate, even though I was not active in politics. During the campaign, I made an expedient decision. I had good intentions, but I was motivated by *fear* of the possibility of losing the election.

I made a *quick* decision "on the spot" to allow some people to send out a mail piece on my behalf. They even paid for all of the associated expenses! In my haste, I failed to:

- Run the idea by my campaign committee. My thinking was that I was the candidate, and I should be making decisions.

- Review and approve the mail piece with my name all over it before it was mailed, or at least let my campaign committee approve it.

- Approve the mail list that the people were going to use.

After the piece was already mailed, I learned:

- The people used a mail piece we would not have approved.

- They got overzealous and expanded the mail list to include potential voters who did not want to receive the mail piece.

Well . . . Even though this bad decision did not ruin my campaign, I spent a lot of time mending fences.

What Are Expedient Behaviors?

Expedient behaviors are those that can be done quickly and easily and will fulfill a person's immediate self-interests. They are done without consideration of what is just, fair, or right for the long term.

If we want to reduce expedient behavior, the first step is to learn how to identify its telltale signs. Every person can identify expedient behavior by recognizing the following characteristics:

- It is (or seems) quick and easy.

- It will give short-term pleasure.

- It is reactive to the current situation.

- It offers short-term gain.

- It is based on self-centeredness or selfishness.

- It gives immediate gratification after the decision is made.

- It is made because of anxiety and insecurity.

- It often indicates the pride of the person making the decision.

Please keep in mind that expedient behavior is rooted in fear. I'm talking about fear that you are going to lose something you don't want to lose, or fear that you are going to experience something you don't want to experience.

The Consequences of Expedient Behavior

When expedient behavior becomes a habit, your life and business suffer unhealthy consequences. The following are examples of the impact and consequences of expediency:

- Many unforeseen errors are found.

- The decision maker(s) and others must rework to find yet another solution.

- Other priorities or aspects are neglected.

- Clients, employees, and others affected by the expedient decision complain about the consequences.

- Conflict arises because of unforeseen complications.

- The decision-maker(s) often experience regret for the expedient decision.

- The outcome fails entirely.

When these unhealthy consequences occur, do you "blow them off" with excuses by blaming someone or something else? Or do you learn from them and change to a principled way of behavior so you can move forward?

Principled behavior may take a little more time and a little more personal restraint. But principled behaviors almost always produce better results than expedient ones.

> Insanity: doing the same thing over and
> over again and expecting different results.
> —UNKNOWN

Pause for Reflection:

1. *How often do you find yourself "mending fences" due to expedient behavior?*

2. *Are you learning from your failures so you can move forward?*

The Hallmarks of Principled Behavior

Two of my young grandsons, who call me "G-Bob" (that stands for Grand-bob) and call my wife "Mimi," were born two years apart from each other—but their birthdays are only one day apart. Since their birthdays are so close, most parents would throw one combined birthday party, right? Wouldn't it make sense to have one party? Yes. Wouldn't it be more convenient for everyone and save time? Yes. In other words, hosting one party for the two boys would be expedient. However, my son and daughter-in-law made a principled decision to have a separate birthday party for each boy.

This year, the older grandson wanted a birthday cake, and the younger grandson wanted birthday cupcakes. At each occasion, we sang "Happy Birthday" and gave the honoree his gifts.

Each grandson felt so important to have all of the attention just on him. Each was "king of the hill," if only for a day. And that was what mattered most—not saving time and effort by combining the parties.

What Are Principled Behaviors?

Every person can identify principled decisions by recognizing the following characteristics and successful results. Keep in mind that principled behaviors are actions based on or consistent with:

- Fundamental beliefs and rules of conduct.

- Long-term appropriateness and effectiveness.

- Self-discipline and willingness to forgo the lure of immediate gratification or tempting shortcuts.

The following are characteristics of principled behavior:

- Requires more time.

- Team centered.

- Analytic.

- Proactive.

- Intentional, sound decisions.

- Sacrificial for the short term.

- Painful for the short term.

- Worthwhile in the long term.

- Secure.

Please keep in mind that principled behavior is rooted in *faith*. Faith that what you want to happen is going to happen, or faith that you are going to experience something you want to experience.

Where there is faith, there is no fear. And where there is fear, there is no faith.

The Results of Principled Behavior

When you consistently make principled decisions, your life and your business eventually experience growth and success. The following are examples of the impact and successful results of principled behavior:

- Reduced risks.

- Fewer errors.

- Less rework.

- Continual progress.

- Lasting gratification.

- Enjoyment and fun.

- Less stress.

- Respect from and for others.

Moment by moment of every day, we are making choices. We have a choice to behave in an expedient way or in a principled way. We can choose to *play now* (in an expedient way) and pay more later or to *pay now* (in a principled way) and play more later. Either way you choose, you still pay!

In fact, since things compound (like compounding interest), if you choose to play now and pay later, you will pay *more* later. The choice is clear.

Though we have the freedom to make choices, we are *not* free to choose the consequences of our choices.

Pause for Reflection:

1. *Would you throw one birthday party or two?*

2. *Which do you prefer . . . to play now and pay more later? Or to pay now and play more later?*

Principled Decisions Yield Long-Term Success

Several years ago, I was enjoying a tasty Texas BBQ lunch with a manager at my company when he said, "Bobby, I've noticed you use the same process to make every decision, no matter if it is a six-pack of Cokes or six thousand cases of Coke." I took that as a compliment about how I made principled decisions, and I thanked him.

He went on, though, to describe a circumstance in which his daughter acted in contradiction to a strong conviction that he held, yet he agreed with her actions. In response to the puzzled look on my face, he said, "Bobby, when it is your daughter, it is different!"

As you can see, he was making an expedient (emotional) decision based on the situation.

One thing I've learned about life is that your emotions, if left unchecked, will always override your intellect.

People who consistently say one thing but do something different choose to behave based on their *emotions* (in an expedient way) rather than on their *character* (in a principled way). People who behave expediently do what's easiest or what makes them the happiest in the *short run*.

People who behave in an expedient way find it more convenient to *react* to the urgent things in life and in business. They are often guided by *emotion* and choose to make popular decisions that are rooted in unhealthy fears. At the same time, they worry about protecting their rights. Emotional decisions made in haste lead to poor outcomes.

Those who are principled think about what is right in the *long run*. They are self-disciplined to do what is right even though it might not be the easiest, quickest, or most enjoyable thing to do!

When faced with situations that might test our *character,* we can use the following information to help us reach principled, character-driven decisions.

Character-Driven People	Emotion-Driven People
Do right, then feel good	Feel good, then do right
Are commitment-driven	Are convenience-driven
Make principle-based decisions	Make popular-based decisions
Action controls attitude	Attitude controls action
Believe it, then see it	See it, then believe it
Create momentum	Wait for momentum
Ask: What are my responsibilities?	Ask: What are my rights?

In short, character-driven people are willing to do things emotion-driven people will not bother to do! Character-driven people enjoy long-term success, while emotion-driven people usually wind up on the road to failure.

Make Better Decisions

Every person can make better decisions by understanding the differences between emotion-driven and character-driven decision making.

People who behave in a principled way make better decisions, as they seek what is right and then hold to those convictions. They are proactive and focus on what is important versus what is urgent in life and business. And they initiate action by filling their calendar with their priorities proactively rather than being acted upon by other people's requests reactively.

Rather than jumping to what looks like a greener pasture on the other side, they first invest in fertilizing the pasture they are in currently. They also choose to trust the process, which leads to principled decisions that are rooted in faith. At the same time, they accept their responsibilities, which come with their rights.

Do you want to make better decisions? It's possible—*if* you focus on making character-driven decisions based on principles, instead of expedient, emotion-driven decisions.

Pause for Reflection:

1. *How do you make decisions?*

2. *Are they based on the situation?*

3. *Are they character driven or emotion driven?*

Examples of Expedient and Principled Behavior

I love eating Krispy Kreme donuts! They are lip-smacking good. Have you eaten a Krispy Kreme donut when it's come out fresh and is still warm? They literally melt in your mouth. Eating a donut requires little discipline. You simply pick your favorite donut (or three), pay for it, and enjoy the deliciousness! It is an expedient, emotional experience. Until you weigh in the next day.

Because I love to eat and because I need a stress reliever, I've made a principled decision to stay active on a regular basis. In fact, I've been exercising six days a week, almost every week, for over thirty years. I have ridden my bicycle about a hundred thousand miles. I've sweated off countless calories while swimming and running. Last year, I even tried CrossFit. These days, I just focus on bicycling and long walks.

Discipline is doing what you don't want to do today so you can do what you want to do tomorrow.

Donut eating and regular exercise are, respectively, personal examples of expedient and principled behavior. But we can use these categories in other areas of our lives. Most of the situations we encounter present us with a choice to act in either an expedient or a principled way. Consider the following examples:

Human Resource Examples

Expedient: Hiring in haste and regretting at leisure.

Principled: Screening applicants carefully and always checking references.

Expedient: Taking a new employee to his or her desk, briefly describing duties, and going back to your daily tasks.

Principled: Providing new employees with ample guidance before giving them assignments.

Expedient: Making quick and easy promises to employees without verifying that the promises can be fulfilled without violating company policies and procedures.

Principled: Checking with your own supervisor before promising or doing anything for a subordinate about his or her employment.

Business Meeting Examples

Expedient: Arriving for meetings at your convenience.

Principled: Considerately arriving on time so others aren't delayed.

Expedient: Holding meetings without prior information about the purpose of the meeting.

Principled: Announcing the purpose of the meeting along with the time and place.

Customer Relations Example

Expedient: Making unrealistic commitments to customers in order to get their agreement to buy.

Principled: Being clear and forthright with customers and prospects regarding the nature and timing of deliverables.

Personal Examples

Expedient: Interrupting others early and frequently without trying to understand what they are saying.

Principled: Listening to others without interrupting.

Expedient: Postponing or avoiding periodic checkups and preventive activities because you have other, more pleasant priorities.

Principled: Taking care of your health and your possessions, such as with periodic physicals for you and oil changes for your vehicles.

Expedient: Doing your own things until you risk being late and then speeding down the streets and intersections.

Principled: Allowing ample time to drive to your destination safely.

Leading and Managing Examples

Expedient: Fire, ready, aim!

Principled: Ready, aim, fire!

Expedient: Continually reacting quickly when things go wrong repetitively.

Principled: Tracking and analyzing patterns of problematic occurrences and designing preventive measures.

Expedient: Deciding or doing something quickly but without checking with others.

Principled: When facing a challenge or opportunity, immediately seeking out people who can help you make a better decision, will have to carry out the decision, or will be impacted by it.

Expedient: As a supervisor or key staff member, doing everything you can in order to stay in control and be sure things are done to your liking.

Principled: Delegating to others whenever possible even though you probably could do it more quickly—and more to your liking—by yourself.

Expedient: Orally giving the same instructions repeatedly each time a challenge or opportunity arises.

Principled: Investing the time to develop helpful systems, procedures, and checklists for repetitive future use.

The above examples of principled decisions require the *faith* and *discipline* to invest in appropriate communication, coordination, and cooperation with others, but the rewards are growth and success!

Pause for Reflection:

1. *Do you like eating donuts? If so, do you exercise to offset the calories?*

2. *Do you have the consistent discipline to make principled decisions?*

3. *Which example from above are you going to put into practice?*

Three Strategies to Help You Make Better Decisions

My wife and I have three sons. They are all adults now, but I remember holding hands with them as we crossed the street when they were little boys. Like most parents, we tried to protect them as best we could and help them avoid physical injury.

Getting physically hurt would have been a tragedy, but there are other risks that are just as dangerous! Fortunately, I discovered some ways to help us stay safe.

From an early age, our boys have heard me talk about doing everything they can to protect their minds. I would say to them, "Your mind is like a computer . . . garbage in is garbage out. You want to protect what your eyes see and what your ears hear."

Those boys knew that I was going to ask them:

- "What kind of music are you listening to?"
- "What movies do you plan to see?"
- "What TV shows are you watching?"
- "What websites are you visiting?"
- "What magazines/books are you reading?"
- "What language do you and your friends use, and what jokes do you tell?"

I would share with them, "When you consistently allow enough garbage to come into your mind, you will eventually begin to live out [in an expedient way] that same garbage, resulting in addiction and consequences." I would continue, "On the other hand, when you more consistently protect what your eyes see and what your ears hear, you will live out [in a principled way] a life with growth, blessings, and success."

You make your choices, and your choices make you!

I use a three-pronged strategy to consistently make principled decisions and avoid the consequences and results of expedient decisions. This strategy applies equally to the business world and to all other areas of life, regardless of whether you are on vacation with your family or negotiating a merger of billion-dollar companies. It is easy to partition our lives into "work," "leisure," "family," and other compartments, but your decisions must be consistently principled in *all* of these areas if you expect them to succeed and thrive. Whether in the privacy of your home or in the seat of power in the corner office, your approach to making decisions will make or break you every time.

Protect Your Mind

We can better understand the importance of protecting our minds when we realize that everything begins with a *thought*.

In his classic book *As a Man Thinketh*, James Allen states, "A man is literally what he thinks, his character being the complete sum of all his thoughts." That can either be a good thing or a bad thing.

One of the reasons people don't achieve their dreams is that they desire to change their *results* (in an expedient way) without changing their *thinking*. You can begin making principled decisions when you implement the "*thinking* for a change" process:

- Think: Ponder what your eyes see and what your ears hear.
- Action: It is said that if you act in a principled way for thirty days, you'll form a habit.
- Habit: A habit will eventually define your character.
- Character: This is who you are.

When you change what you think, you change what you do, and you change who you are!

Know Your Core Values

Another key to making principled decisions is to evaluate opportunities in light of your core values. I have found that once I discovered my core values (who I was) and had them written down, it became easier to consistently make principled decisions.

Insight: When the employees in our company knew our core values, it also became easier as a *team* to consistently make principled decisions.

When your people understand and live out changeless core values (*who* you are) along with the organization's purpose (*why* you exist), they will overcome the change going on all around them in the workplace and marketplace.

Why? Because you have created in your people's hearts and minds a frame of reference, a set of criteria or guidelines, by which they can *govern themselves*.

In chapter 6 of this book, we'll dig into the important topic of core values.

Prepare a Plan

When you are faced with a choice between making a principled decision or an expedient one, you should:

- Pause, slow down, and breathe.
- Get in the habit of "sleeping on it" by waiting overnight before you make your final decision.

- Get wise counsel. If you are married, also ask your spouse.

- Create a T-chart, and list the pros down one side of the paper and the cons on the other side.

- Ask questions, and listen.

One of the best tools I have used to ask questions is the Rotary Club's guide for personal and professional relationships. It's called The Four-Way Test,[2] and it can be used to guide the things we think, say, and do:

1. Is it the TRUTH?

2. Is it FAIR to all concerned?

3. Will it build GOODWILL and BETTER FRIENDSHIPS?

4. Will it be BENEFICIAL to all concerned?

When we protect our minds, know our values, and prepare a plan, we'll be positioned to make better decisions!

Pause for Reflection:

1. *What do you do to protect your mind?*

2. *Are you willing to change your behavior in order to make better decisions? (Remember, changed thinking always precedes changed behavior!)*

---

[2] "Guiding Principles," Rotary International, https://www.rotary.org/en/guiding-principles.

CHAPTER FIVE:
A Mindset That Creates Success

ENERGIZE YOUR LEADERSHIP WITH
AN ABUNDANCE MINDSET

"Abundance thinkers believe there is always more
where that came from."

MICHAEL HYATT

S ince I was a young boy, people have asked me, "Why do you smile so much?"

At one time, I would answer, "I don't know." However, over the years, I have come to know that my smile comes from a grateful heart.

When I look over my life, I don't have any regrets. Have I made mistakes? Yes. Have I ever had a time when I was very disappointed? Yes. Still, somehow I have always learned from my mistakes, overcome disappointments, and moved forward. Even if I make a mistake, instead of dwelling on it, my thinking usually goes to considering my next options.

I realized that my perspective comes from principled decisions supported by an abundance mindset.

An Abundance Mindset

People with an abundance mindset view their resources as a farmer views seeds. A successful farmer liberally sows seeds, trying to ensure a good fall harvest. He believes in the principle of sowing and reaping: the more he sows, the more he reaps.

Successful leaders and people with an abundance mindset see their resources as sufficient (plentiful) seeds to be sown. They know the harvest will come and more will be created.

You can't harvest if you haven't planted.

A Scarcity Mindset

Some leaders find it hard to invest resources because they feel so deficient. These leaders think with a scarcity mindset. They always feel (in an expedient way) that their commodities are about to run out. Consequently, people with a scarcity mindset tend to be protective of what they have and what they know. Their mindset encourages them to be selfish with their time, talent, and money.

A Contrast in Mindsets

Consider the differences between the scarcity mindset and the abundance mindset.

Abundance Mindset	Scarcity Mindset
Proactive	Reactive
Offensive	Defensive
Dynamic: Let go!	Paralyzed: Hold on!
Pursue Vision	Prevent Loss
Create	Maintain
Think Win/Win	Think Win/Lose
Risk & Seize Opportunity	Guard & Protect Position

John Maxwell talks about the gap between two significant questions:

- "Can I?" A question asked by those who have a scarcity mindset.
- "How can I?" A question asked by those who have an abundance mindset.

Which question do you most often ask?

The more we understand the differences between an abundance mindset and a scarcity mindset, the more likely we'll make principled decisions from a place of *abundance!*

Pause for Reflection:

1. *Do you smile when you meet people?*

2. *Do you ask, "Can I?" or "How can I?"*

3. *Will you approach your next challenge or opportunity with the question, "How can I?"*

Why Abundant Thinkers Succeed with Flying Colors!

I wish I had Superman underwear like my grandsons do! It reminds me of when I was a little boy. I would watch Superman on TV, and he would always say, "Up, up, and away!" right before he took flight! After watching Superman, I would pretend to have his superhero powers—flying faster than a speeding bullet and leaping tall buildings in a single bound.

I learned five truths from that TV series:

- Be content with who you are, even though you may be different.

- Be a person with strong character qualities.

- Teach your children to behave in a principled way, and model this in your own behavior.

- Use your gifts to benefit others and to protect others from those who use evil means and are self-centered.

- Always have a *positive* abundance mindset.

Insight: People with an abundance mindset believe that today's *short-term* pain, sacrifice, and investment in time, energy, and money will eventually bring *long-term* growth, blessings, and success.

It turns out that people who adopt an abundance mindset approach life, challenges, and opportunities in a principled manner that literally paves the way for them to succeed.

The following are examples of Abundant Thinkers and Scarcity Thinkers.

Enough for Everyone

Abundant Thinkers know there is enough in the world for everyone to share in a piece of the pie. They understand that the more you share in a principled way, the more the abundance grows.

Scarcity Thinkers believe there is not enough of anything to go around. They fear that there will not be enough for them, especially if they share with others.

Don't Compare with Others

Abundant Thinkers don't compare themselves with others—only with themselves. They set realistic goals and then work to achieve them. They encourage others to do the same. Their goals are based (in a principled way) upon a logical study of achievable results in each step.

Scarcity Thinkers continually ask themselves why they aren't like others or why they do not have the things others have. If the "others" are younger, or prettier or more handsome, they are perceived to have an advantage.

In the workplace, these types of supervisors lead in an expedient way by keeping their workers subservient, since equality would be viewed as competition.

Win-Win

Abundant Thinkers find common ground with their colleagues. They know that unresolved conflict is wasted time and energy and subtracts from an abundant environment. They see *win-win* and assume that there is a way for all concerned to profit and thrive. They understand that constructive criticism (in a principled way) helps others to *grow*.

Scarcity Thinkers want to be at the center of attention because they want all they can get for themselves. They know (sometimes unconsciously) that for this to happen, others have to *lose*. They think that if they can use expedient means to get something done more *quickly*, their "win" justifies their "survival of the fittest" approach.

Gratitude

Abundant Thinkers live lives of *gratitude* for the abundance of the world in which they live. They are positive and upbeat. To them, life is a continuously replenished bowl of fruit—all ripe for the taking. They teach others how to be positive and live in gratitude.

Scarcity Thinkers are *not* grateful for what they have. They see their life's accomplishments as the result of only their hard work and are unable to give heartfelt thanks to others for helping.

In the workplace, these types of thinkers teach their followers that life's abundance is *limited*, so they had better do what they need to do to grab (in an expedient way) the brass ring.

Give Time, Talent, and Treasures

Abundant Thinkers know that giving their time, talent, and treasures will come back to them in so many ways, thus increasing the abundance in their own lives. This principled process strengthens and fosters team building and creative thinking that supports continual improvement.

Scarcity Thinkers do not share. After all, they are driven by a deep-seated belief (in an expedient way) that there isn't enough to go around, so they cannot afford to give anything away. They truly believe that if they share their knowledge or wealth, they will lose power and possessions both now and in the future.

The freedom and success enjoyed by Abundant Thinkers becomes obvious when we contrast it with the limiting beliefs of Scarcity Thinkers. Just like Kryptonite affects Superman, scarcity thinking weakens our effectiveness and keeps us from realizing our full potential. But a perspective of abundance ensures that there's always enough to go around and keeps us moving forward.

Pause for Reflection:

1. *Do you have an abundance mindset or a scarcity mindset?*

2. *What challenge or opportunity are you facing today that would benefit from a shift toward an abundance mindset?*

PART IV
CORE VALUES

CHAPTER SIX:
Discover and Build Your Core

---

*"It's not hard to make decisions when
you know what your values are."*

ROY DISNEY

T oday, people worldwide enjoy the products and experiences that bear the name Disney. Fewer people know, however, the many changes and trials that the company has passed through, starting when Walt Disney first moved to Los Angeles in 1923 and tried—without success—to find a job in the movie business. Walt and his brother Roy formed their own studio, but repeated setbacks followed, including the devastating loss of most of their animators and the rights to their first hit character to another studio. Walt Disney Productions persevered, and in 1937, it produced the first successful full-length animated feature: *Snow White and the Seven Dwarfs*. It was a milestone for cinematic history, and for Disney, who continued to produce popular and award-winning films and also branched into television. In the 1950s, after visiting a number of theme parks and feeling they fell far short of their potential, Walt expressed his desire for a place where children and parents could enjoy time together. The end result was a new kind of theme park, one where millions of people have now shared the wonder and magic of childhood. Disneyland became an amazing success, as did Walt Disney, who earned more than 950 honors—including forty-eight Academy Awards—and established a legacy that endures to this day.

In *Good to Great,* Jim Collins discusses the reason behind the Disney company's extraordinary and enduring success: "Throughout all these dramatic changes—from cartoons to full-length feature animation, from the *Mickey Mouse Club* to Disney World—the company held firmly to a consistent set of core values that included passionate belief in creative imagination, fanatic attention to detail, abhorrence of cynicism, and preservation of the 'Disney Magic.'"

I believe that the unprecedented success of Walt Disney is available to anyone. Anyone, that is, who anchors his or her efforts with an unchanging set of core values. Those values become a beacon that illuminates and defines how we pursue our purpose and our vision. As Walt's brother put it, it's not hard to make decisions when you know what your values are.

Leading with Core Values

Are you ready to create a frame of reference—a set of criteria and guidelines that will clearly show your people *how* to think and conduct themselves—in their hearts and minds? Would you like to lead a dynamic team that reflects your values and accomplishes their work with less direction and oversight?

The questions above reveal the desires of almost every leader I've encountered. After answering those questions with a hearty yes, we then ask, "But how?"

Based on years of study and my own experience leading businesses, I can share with you that the answer is to identify your authentic core values and then to communicate them to your people and instill them into the very fabric of your organization.

I have been asked a very insightful and important question: Can core values be learned? From what I have observed, they *cannot* be learned. Core values reflect who you are. They are not a skill you can learn. You cannot give what you do not have.

Although core values cannot be learned, you can indeed discover your own core values!

Roy Disney was right—making decisions becomes much easier when you know your values. This simple statement gives hope to everyone. Surviving and thriving in business has its share of challenges, but when you know your core values, you know what to do and how you need to do it! When your people buy into changeless core values (*who* you are) along with the organization's purpose (*why* you exist), they will be able to navigate the choppy and changing waters of the marketplace with clarity and confidence.

Pause for Reflection:

1. *Are you ready to discover "who you are"?*

Confronting the problem does not always bring a solution, but until you confront a problem, there can be no solution.

—JAMES BALDWIN, PARAPHRASED BY ZIG ZIGLAR

CORE VALUES: THE PROBLEM
The Cycle of Self-Defeat

Have you ever felt a sense of guilt because you couldn't make things work? You think you can make progress if you just try harder. Then you become fatigued. And then you want to quit. Finally, the cycle starts over again, and again, and again, but you never get anywhere.

Author John Ortberg calls this the "Cycle of Self-Defeat" in his book *The Me I Want to Be*. It is a very real phenomenon. And it can have crippling results if it isn't disrupted.

When my father died at fifty-seven years old, his abrupt passing meant that I became the new leader of the family business. So there I was, twenty years old, leading five employees, all of whom were older than me. Plus, I discovered that the business was carrying a huge amount of debt.

In those early years, it was very hard to make it all work. Over time, I learned what to focus on for success. Perhaps as crucial, though, was learning what to avoid. I believe that every leader can escape the Cycle of Self-Defeat by focusing on core values and avoiding the following leadership traps.

Leadership Trap #1: Focusing on the Wrong Things

There are some common misconceptions about leadership. What some people see as "good leadership" does, in fact, limit the effectiveness of the leader and the success of the organization.

I often thought that emphasizing certain *things* would help my leadership and my company. I learned, however, to avoid doing the following:

- Embracing fads and engaging management hoopla aimed at "motivating the troops" rather than confronting the brutal facts.

- Using a crisis to persuade "unmotivated" employees to accept the need for change.

- Thinking that success was reached through brilliant and complex strategies.

- Focusing on beating the competition as a primary business-growth strategy.

- Making a major acquisition as a way to increase growth and diversify away from the current troubles of the organization.

- Defining profit or shareholder wealth as the first and foremost goal of the organization.

Leadership Trap #2: Focusing on the Wrong People Matters

People are the engine of any organization. When you stop and think about it, they are also the heart and soul of what you are trying to achieve.

Here's some wrong thinking about people that can limit your leadership and the success of your company:

- Jumping right into action *before* you get the right people on the bus, the wrong people off the bus, and the right people in the right seats.

- Thinking that a high-profile, charismatic leader will solve the organization's problems.

- Introducing fear-driven change; using the fear of seeing others win or the fear of encountering monumental failure. (Fear doesn't effectively drive change, but it does perpetuate mediocrity.)

- Assuming that the values and guiding principles of another successful company should be adopted as your own set of core values. (The core values of an organization are unique. They are reflected in and through its people and, most importantly, through its leader.)

It all boils down to *things* and *people*. Are you focused on the right things? Are you attentive to the people in your organization?

You might be stuck in the Cycle of Self-Defeat, but you can break it by learning who you are. And knowing who you are starts with understanding your core values.

Pause for Reflection:

1. *How have you sidestepped some of the traps listed above?*

2. *Have you gotten stuck in a cycle of self-defeat? If so, how did you escape? Which of the traps listed above have limited your effectiveness as leader?*

CORE VALUES: THE SOLUTION
The First Step to Success

For years, I have read books about business and leadership, including Tom Peters's book *In Search of Excellence* in 1989. I did not know it at the time, but that book started me on a journey that would ultimately transform the way I ran my business.

One of my main takeaways from the book was the importance of a company's beliefs. I was so moved by this concept that I pulled some ideas from the book and compiled our own statement of beliefs. This new statement, entitled "Our Beliefs," contained eight key beliefs that I'd gleaned from the book.

As the years went by, whenever we had company-wide meetings, I would go over "Our Beliefs" with our people. I understood we needed to be reminded of them, and we always had new people who had come onboard and had not yet heard them before.

Something Was Wrong

My leadership team and I would highlight "Our Beliefs" at our company-wide meetings. As a leader, I knew it was my job to define and champion the beliefs and purpose of the organization. But something stirring within me gave me a sense that "Our Beliefs" were not right. I stopped using "Our Beliefs" at our meetings because I knew something was missing.

A Clue

In the fall of 2004, during the nonpeak season of our business, our leadership team was doing our annual book review to stimulate personal growth. We reviewed the book *Good to Great* by Jim Collins, in which Collins explained his research into how *good* companies could make the leap to become *great* companies. Collins had discovered that core values were key to an organization's success.

> **Leadership Tip: Use nonpeak times to turn your focus inward in order to grow yourself and your team.**

He explained that our company's core values needed to reflect "who I was" as the leader of the organization. He also said, "Core values are essential for enduring greatness, but it doesn't seem to matter what those core values are." The point is that there is not a single right set of core values found in all successful companies. Rather, you must do the hard work of identifying the honorable values that are true to you and your company, intentionally weaving them into the very fabric of your organization, and taking care to preserve them over time.

I was beginning to sense that this concept of core values was related to my failed attempt at the company's "Our Beliefs." At this stage, I had a lot more to learn, both about myself and about the importance of core values.

A Question

Leading and growing an organization can be downright hard. Still, any journey starts with the first step, and I discovered that the first step to success starts with a question. Could I ask you perhaps the most important question you've ever been asked?

Who are you? Bone deep, who are you?

Your answer may have more impact on your business and your life than anything else!

Pause for Reflection:

1. *Do you know who you really are?*

What Core Values Are (And What They're Not!)

You know when you run into someone from high school and the conversation just pulls you back to your teenage years? Even hearing a song from our youth can stir up thoughts and feelings from decades gone by. The experiences, thoughts, and actions from our pasts can reveal some interesting clues about who we are, bone deep.

Early in my quest to identify my own values, I began looking over my life and thinking back to when I was a little boy. My purpose was to tap the power of introspection to determine, "Who am I?"

Have you ever tried to look at yourself introspectively to figure out "who you are"? I can tell you that it was not an easy process. I wasn't used to this level of thinking about myself.

I learned that this exercise is not a "knock it out in one morning" type of task. It is more like peeling back an onion, one layer at a time. Determining your core values is a *process*, not an *event*. I also learned that you do not "set" your core values. You have to (and can) *discover* them!

Every leader can discover who he or she is by understanding the following three fundamental truths.

What Core Values Are

I like Jim Collins's definition of core values: "Core values are the organization's essential and enduring tenets—a small set of general guiding principles; not to be confused with specific cultural or operating practices; not to be compromised for financial gain or short-term expediency." This is indeed a small set; I have learned that most people or organizations only have three to six core values.

What Core Values Are NOT

The process to discover your core values is *not* figuring out what:

- Maximizes your wealth.
- Sounds good to yourself or others.
- Reflects your aspirations.
- Complements your marketing campaign.
- Pleases the financial community.
- Looks attractive printed on glossy paper.
- Echoes popular opinion.
- Appeals to outsiders.

What Finding Your Core Values Requires

Discovering your core values requires:

- *Authenticity.* Getting real, with nothing added for public agreement.

- *Introspective reflection.* What do I stand for? What am I all about?

- *Articulating what is inside, bone deep.* Those things that are as natural as breathing.

- *Patience.* Although many managers miss this point as they drive for results, this is a discovery process that takes time, not a single event to be knocked out in a day.

What Your Sleep Reveals about Your Leadership

What keeps you up at night? When I was president and CEO of our company, I had four main issues that would often keep me up or wake me up at night: people, money/financing, government regulations, and changing sales processes.

I learned that I could not control most of these challenges. But I *could* control how I responded concerning them. And how I responded had everything to do with my core values.

Once I discovered "who I was," I had more peace when dealing with issues that I could and could not control. Also, I began to sleep great at night. And you can, too!

Every leader can benefit from listing and thinking about their top problems or concerns. Think about your current situation and honestly answer these questions:

1. What are the top two challenges (in business or in life) that you are facing right now?

2. What problem or challenge did you spend the most time dealing with yesterday?

Insight: Core values are driven by the founder, owner, president, or leader of an organization's division or department. And the core values must be *discovered* by the leader, *not* "set."

For most leaders, as your business goes, so goes your sleep—or lack thereof! Think about your own sleep patterns as we look at three types of organizations and the degree of sleep associated with each type.

Sleepless Nights

Most organizations are being led by a leader who does *not* know "who they are." Therefore, the employees do not know who they are.

The employees don't know how they are to behave with customers, suppliers, and with their coworkers.

Since employees are hired with such a various and diverse set of core values, there is a lack of cohesiveness and unity of spirit. Without a common set of core values, there is little teamwork to make the dream work.

It is sad that most of these organizations work very hard every day and try to do the right thing. But they are underperforming financially. And they don't even know *why*.

A Better Night's Sleep

A small number of organizations are being led by leaders who *do* know "who they are." The core values were announced at a short, one-time meeting. Those values may even be on a plaque as you enter the office.

That's it. And I mean—that's it.

The employees may remember hearing about the core values when they were announced. But they could *not* tell you what they are or even what they mean.

Therefore, the employees don't understand *how* they should behave when interacting with and connecting with customers, suppliers, and their coworkers. Neither are there systems in place to assure alignment of core values. In fact, incentives or bonuses may even encourage employees to violate one or more core values.

Financially, these organizations are performing OK. But if they only knew what they were missing, they could knock the ball out of the park! How? Let's look at the next type of organization.

A Great Night's Sleep

**A culture of discipline is not just about action.
It is about getting disciplined people
who engage in disciplined thought and
who then take disciplined action.**

—JIM COLLINS

Jim Collins is saying that when you have disciplined people—people who are intentional and guided by the *same* core values—you produce superior results.

And it starts with hiring practices: hiring people of the same core values.

Leaders of this type of organization have learned what is more important than a powerful strategy, a super product, or the newest technology. It is an organization of people with the same core values.

And these people know *how* to behave as they pursue the organization's purpose, vision, strategies, tactics, and performance goals.

These organizations substantially outperform all others.

Pause for Reflection:

1. *What is keeping you up at night?*

CORE VALUES: THE BENEFITS
The Key to Extraordinary Growth

In February 2005, while I was attending my monthly CEO group meeting at the CEO Institute, one of the CEOs said something that prompted me to write down this statement: "I want to be a values-driven company that achieves results, not a results-driven company that has values." That statement shook me, and it was exactly what I was looking for. But even after I jotted it down, I still did not know who I was, bone deep.

What I have now learned is that *every* company has values, even if they haven't been discovered yet. I have also found that most companies are results driven and *not* values driven.

> I want to be a values-driven company that achieves results, not a results-driven company that has values.

Three Types of Companies

Not long after that February 2005 meeting, our leadership team wanted to do a review on the book *Built to Last* by Jim Collins and Jerry Porras. In the book, Collins and Porras looked at some of the United States' most successful corporations, many of which date back to the 1800s. Using decades of data and exacting criteria for evaluation, Collins and Porras compared three distinct groups of organizations:

- **Visionary companies:** the best of the best, described as "premier institutions in their industries, widely admired by their peers and having a long track record of making a significant impact on the world around them."

- **Comparison companies:** close competitors to the visionary companies who have achieved a high level of success, but not to the extent of the visionary companies.

- **Average companies:** as represented by the average performance of companies in the general stock market.

Extraordinary Results

What is amazing is the extraordinary long-term financial performance of these enduring, great, visionary companies. Collins and Porras contrasted the three types of companies by showing what $1 invested on January 1, 1926, would grow to by December 31, 1990. Here's what they found:

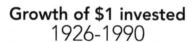

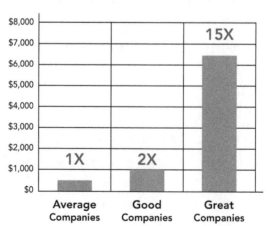

**Growth of $1 invested
1926-1990**

From 1926 to 1990, your investment in the good, "comparison" companies would have earned two times more than the general stock market, which is pretty good. But your investment in the enduring, great visionary companies would have been *fifteen times greater* than the general stock market.

Wow! So what makes these visionary companies different? For that matter, why do only a few companies have extraordinary profits, while the rest never make it to the top level of competition? What do these super successful companies know that the rest of us do not?

I asked myself these questions when I was trying to grow our business. And the answers I found should bring hope to *any* struggling organization!

Shocking Fact: Visionary companies are generally more ideologically driven and less purely profit driven.

Preserve the Core and Stimulate Progress

Collins and Porras discovered that the enduring, great visionary companies did a couple of things very well. The authors summed it up by stating that visionary companies *"Preserved the Core and Stimulated Progress."* This meant the organization's Core Ideology—which they define as core values plus purpose—was always fanatically protected and never changed while they "stimulated progress" by endlessly adapting their business and operating practices.

Over time, these visionary companies changed almost everything: policies, procedures, product lines, competencies, organization structure, reward systems, strategies, tactics, and performance goals. But the *one thing* they did not change was their Core Ideology.

The Albert Companies

At our company, we were definitely not perfect, but over time, we got more intentional about creating a great and enduring company. From 2005 (the fall I introduced our company core values) through 2011 (the year I sold our company), we saw the following results during some of the toughest economic times:

- Revenue grew about five times.

- Profit increased slightly more than five times.

- EBITDA (Earnings Before Interest, Taxes, Depreciation, and Amortization) increased about five times.

- We were awarded the 100 Best Companies to Work For in Texas distinction in 2011 and 2012.

Our company experienced significant growth during a time when many other companies were declining. And so can yours! I believe that every leader can create a top-performing organization by focusing on the two areas Collins and Porras identified: preserving the core and stimulating progress. A major key to this is discovering your core values so you can be a values-driven company that achieves results, not a results-driven company that has values.

Pause for Reflection:

1. *Are you a RESULTS-driven company that has values or a VALUES-driven company that achieves results?*

2. *Would you like to be a values-driven company?*

CORE VALUES: THE DISCOVERY PROCESS

My Core Values Journey

You may be asking, "What would make my company a visionary company?" The best way to approach answering that question is to share my own experience. While we are all on different paths, our journeys are the same in many ways, so as you read this, consider how your steps to discovering your core values can be modeled on mine.

Key Steps Along the Way

Sometimes, leaders get that feeling in their gut that something isn't right. Have you ever experienced that feeling? Well, in early 2005, I knew that something wasn't right. I had a growing sense that I needed to figure out who I was, bone deep. As our leadership team reviewed Collins and Porras's book, I got serious about answering the question, "Who am I?" For months, I found myself thinking about it when I went to bed, when I got up in the morning, while I was bicycling or on long walks, while in the shower, while driving to work, and on and on. If you have ever wrestled with issues of identity, you know how challenging and consuming they can become. I discovered two steps that anyone can take to help answer this important question.

Step 1: Start by Reflecting

Looking over my life and thinking back to when I was a very little boy, I began to ask myself questions like:

- What do I stand for?
- What am I all about?

I don't know about you, but these questions were some of the most difficult questions I had ever considered.

Step 2: Then Go Deeper

As I went through my days, my antenna was up, and I was continually observing and asking myself the following questions:

- Why did I say what I just said?

- Why was it important for me to say it that way?

- Why did I do what I just did?

- Why was that important for me to do it that way?

Next, I started to reflect about my past by asking questions like:

- Who, even from an early age, influenced what I said and did?

- When did they influence me?

- Where did they influence me?

- How was I affected by these influencers?

I still did not fully know who I was. But I finally got a breakthrough! By asking those questions, I was beginning to understand a few things about myself—characteristics that I could trace back to my childhood. I was learning that there is something inside me that is expressed in my passions, which I identified—through introspective struggle—as a thirst for learning; a focus on honesty, making the right decision regardless of the consequences; a need to lift others up so I can serve them better; a determination to always perform to the best of my ability; a priority of *people* above things; and a desire to positively impact the lives of others.

I was making progress, but I still had not fully and completely discovered who I was.

> *Pause for Reflection:*
>
> 1. *What would happen if you asked yourself the same questions that I asked?*

Two Questions to Help You Discover Your Core Values

Do you have a thinking chair? For as long as I can remember, I've had a chair that I call my thinking chair. It's my favorite chair in the whole house. This chair is where I go to think, to reflect, to evaluate. I vividly remember what happened in my thinking chair on a sunny afternoon one day in June 2005.

On this Sunday afternoon, I sat down in my thinking chair. I don't know how to explain it, but I was finally ready to discover who I was. The afternoon revolved around two simple questions, and I think so highly of these questions that I believe every person can discover who he or she is by asking them.

First Question

I grabbed a pen and a pad of paper and asked the following question of myself to get started: What are the things that I have a passion for, things that I get excited about, and things that give me energy? I wrote down some words that came to my mind as I thought about this question. These words formed a list down the left side of the page.

Second Question

Then I thought about looking on the "other side of the coin" and asked myself the following question: What are the things that, when left un-done, make me angry, frustrated, upset, and even foaming at the mouth?

Then I jotted some words down on the right side of the page in answer to that question.

The entire page contained about thirty words.

As I continued to think about these questions and reviewed the two lists, I realized that there were similar words on both sides of the page. I circled the matching words and came up with six words that showed up on both lists.

Core Values Emerge!

When I looked at those circled words, it hit me—this was "who I am"! These two simple questions had helped me uncover my true core values. The six words common to both lists were:

- Personal Growth
- Integrity
- Add-Value
- Excellence
- Relationships
- Significance

I was able to finally discover who I was *only* after spending weeks and months going through the process of thinking and reflecting on the questions in the previous section.

It's Your Turn

Isn't it interesting that these two very different questions yielded several similar ideas?

What if these same two questions hold the key to unlocking *your* core values? What might happen if you set aside time to really think about these two questions and then took time to reflect on your answers?

I've learned that everyone must discover his or her own core values. My list is not *the* list of values—we each have a *unique* set.

Pause for Reflection:

1. *What is one of your core values?*

2. *Have you considered how the two questions above can help you in your own core values journey?*

Champions Are Made in the Process, Not the Event

In 2016, the Super Bowl had a peak viewing audience of 115.5 million people! It has become the most-watched American television program in history. The Super Bowl game is a wonderful annual event, and the two teams there have gone through a very lengthy season (a process) to arrive at the event. The people preparing for the event have spent months and even years (a process) to prepare for it.

Leadership develops daily, not in a day.

—JOHN C. MAXWELL

John Maxwell shares that the *event* encourages decisions, motivates people, is a calendar issue, challenges people, and is easy. However, John also explains that the *process* encourages development, matures people, is a cultural issue, changes people, and is difficult.

We tend to overestimate the event and underestimate the process. Events are important, and it's easy for us to focus on them, but the secret to winning is found in the process!

Insight: Champions are always made out of the process.

This is why the discovery process of finding your core values is so important. And while core values are essential, not everyone shares the same set of them. The point is not what core values you have but that you know what they are, that you acknowledge them, that you (as the leader) build them explicitly into the organization, and that you preserve them over time.

Validate Your Core Values

Imagine you, the leader, want to recreate a successful, high-quality organization with the very best attributes, but on *another planet*. Yet you only have enough seats on the rocket ship for five people. Whom would you send?

You would most likely choose people who:

- Are exemplars of the organization's core values and purpose.

- Have the highest level of credibility with their peers.

- Possess the highest levels of competence.

But how can you be sure you have identified your core values? Jim Collins developed the following questions to qualify whether a value is truly "core." If you answer with a resounding and unqualified, "Yes!" to *all* seven questions, you're looking at a core value!

1. Industry Independent

If you were to start a new organization, would you build it around this value regardless of the industry?

Your core values are unique to "who you are" regardless of what industry you are in or what product or service you offer. In fact, the leaders of many enduring, great, visionary companies decided their core values before they even knew what products or services they were going to offer.

2. One Hundred Years Strong

Would you want your organization to continue to stand for this value one hundred years into the future, no matter what changes occur in the outside world?

Over time, visionary companies change almost everything, such as policies, procedures, product lines, competencies, organization structure, reward systems, strategies, tactics, and performance goals. But since core values are "who you are," the same companies stand firm on their values and do not allow them to change over time.

3. Against All Odds

Would you want your organization to hold this value even if, at some point in time, it became a competitive disadvantage—even if, in some instances, the environment penalized the organization for living out this value?

From my own leadership experience, I have found that when I've stood on what I believed and what I considered to be the right thing, I have *always* been rewarded and *never* felt I was put to a competitive disadvantage.

Here's an example. Even though I knew I could lose one of our company's largest corporate customers, I confronted them over an integrity issue that also violated one of their own values. They eventually changed their position on the matter to align with our mutual values.

4. Wrong Bus

Do you believe that those who do not share this value—those who breach it consistently—simply do not belong in your organization?

Collins writes about getting "the wrong people off the bus." He does not mean necessarily that these people are *bad* people. He simply means they do not fit your organization and need to move on to another "bus," or organization, that fits them and where they can flourish.

5. Even If

Would you personally continue to hold this value even if you were not rewarded for holding it?

This is about "who you are," *not* whether you are going to be rewarded or not. Our core values transcend compensation, profits, and recognition.

6. More Than a Job

Would you change jobs before giving up this value?

Every person wants to have a sense of purpose and accomplishment. The best way this occurs is when you get on the "right bus" with *disciplined* people of the *same* core values, and you are sitting in the "right seat" on that bus.

7. Lifelong

If you awoke tomorrow with more than enough money to retire comfortably for the rest of your life, would you continue to apply this value to your productive activities?

I am personally in this position right now as I begin my second half of life. One of my core values and passions is to "achieve significance." There is something inside me that drives me to make a positive difference in people, for people, and through people. That's why I'm writing, speaking, teaching, and consulting based on my experiences.

Final Checkup

People frequently confuse timeless core values—what you truly believe and have always believed, bone deep—with aspirations of what you or the organization desires to be like. Aspirations can help you define your strategic vision of the future. But core values address *how* you think and behave and *who* you are as you live and work.

Mixing future aspirations into your authentic core values could create justifiable cynicism in an organization and destroy the power of your core values. Yet when you validate your values, you can be confident they are truly "core."

Pause for Reflection:

1. *With each of your core values, can you answer these seven questions with a resounding and unqualified yes?*

2. *If you can't, you may need to reconsider whether it is truly core.*

Why the Leader?

Now, at this point you may be asking, "Why must it be the leader?"

In the area of discovering the core values that will lead and define an organization, the leader's responsibility is singularly essential. Over time, employees will come and go, but the leader and his or her legacy will remain.

Is each employee being asked to ignore his or her own core values in life and substitute these values for those of the company leader? Should thousands of employees alter their lives and behavior to match one person's set of values?

Absolutely not! As Jim Collins explained in his books *Built to Last* and *Good to Great*, the visionary companies that outperformed the stock market by fifteen times had founders who established their core values at the very beginning. They then went about recruiting, selecting, hiring, and onboarding employees who held the same core values. They hired the right people—those of like core values—and put them in the right positions. They did not have employees with a diverse set of core values. Instead, they developed a unique, consistent culture of remarkable unity, one where people lived out a shared set of core values and purpose.

Even though it was not until October 2005 that my company memorialized our core values in writing as "Our Values," those values were always present. Why? I was authentically living them out even though I had not put them in writing. And our human resource department hired people who fit what the leader (me) wanted in our organization.

I have observed that when my company hired an employee who did not truly share our core values, that new employee learned very quickly that he or she did not fit in our organization and chose to leave. They weren't bad people; they just knew they did not fit. And our other employees knew it as well.

Much like a dropped object is controlled by the law of gravity, a company's values are subject to the law of values origin: the authentic core values of an organization originate and flow from the leader. And the leader must champion them in his or her organization. This is why leadership that puts the good of other people first is so important.

The Danger of Value Cards

"Warning! Warning! Warning! Danger, Will Robinson!" That was what the robot, his arms flying up and down in the air, would say to the young boy in the TV series *Lost in Space*.

When I was a young boy, I really enjoyed that series and related to Will Robinson because I wanted to be an astronaut. Just like Will, we can encounter danger, too. Right now, I'm waving my arms up and down in an effort to warn you about the dangers of using a commonly available values-identification tool.

All leaders can avoid some likely pitfalls if they resist the temptation to take a shortcut in the journey required to discover their core values. I consider the use of "value cards" to be one such shortcut! Run in the opposite direction when someone suggests that you use "value cards" to discover your values.

> ## While the users of these cards are no doubt sincere, I believe the cards should come with a warning from the surgeon general: WARNING! Use this product at your own risk!

So what are value cards, how are they used, and why not use them?

What Are Value Cards?

- They are a tool. The cards contain words describing values that are important to some people.

- They usually cost from twenty dollars to over one hundred. Some are offered for free.

- The decks range from about fifty cards to over three hundred cards.

- Yes, there is some science behind the words on the cards.

How Are They Used?

You sort these cards into several piles depending on how important each one is to you. The ones that seem to hold the most value are placed in the "most important" pile, all the way down to the cards that are the least important to you, which are placed in the "not important" pile. As you sort and rank the cards, you ultimately narrow your focus to the "most important" cards, which are said to represent your values.

Why Not Use Them?

When we are presented with a lot of great values listed for our review, we tend to select values that have a certain appeal versus actually identifying our own, bone-deep values. There can be a big difference between what we aspire to be and who we are.

Furthermore, discovering our values requires a *process*, transpiring over weeks or months, to understand "Who am I?" This process should not be rushed into one session with value cards (an *event*).

There's additional risk when you gather your leadership team, who may have a variety of core values, into a conference room for a single values-discovery event.

Also, leaders are always trying to save time! You may see the value cards as a great way to "get 'er done" so you can move on to the next burning issue. Life is filled with bad decisions that were made with good intentions but misguided expedience. Some things just take time. Discovering your authentic core values is one of them.

A Bigger Principle

There is a bigger principle at work here, and its implications extend beyond a simple deck of value cards. *Any* tool (manual or electronic) that presents the values seeker with a collection or list of sample values is a problem. One example is an online values assessment that presents you with a list of possible values and asks you to select the ones that describe you. It is quite difficult to discover your values in this way because of our natural inclination to select the values that "sound" like great values instead of truly discovering the values that reflect who you are.

Pause for Reflection:

1. *Have you ever used "value cards" or a similar tool to find your core values?*

2. *What was the outcome of that experience?*

3. *Do you sense the core values you found by using "value cards" or "value tools" are truly authentic?*

CORE VALUES: A SUCCESS STORY

On August 23, 1937, two freshly graduated young engineers met to brainstorm ideas for founding a new company together. They discussed their interest in the design and manufacture of products in the field of electrical engineering, but the specifics of *what* they would manufacture were set aside for a later time. They had more important things to discuss, such as the principles that would drive their business. At another meeting, they developed a long list of possibilities: phonograph amplifiers, welding equipment, television receivers, public address systems, and even medical equipment. If they could make a technical contribution, then that product was on the table. Contract projects provided early work, including an electronic machine that supposedly jiggled and shocked its users into losing weight. Their first big revenues came when they sold eight units of audio oscillators—to Walt Disney, in fact.

Jim Collins has shared how he told the story of these two young men while teaching a class on entrepreneurship at the Stanford Graduate School of Business in the early 1990s. He read the founding notes from that 1937 meeting to his class, leaving out the names of the founders, and then challenged his students to rate this start-up on a scale of 1 (low) to 10 (high). The average score was about a three, with Collins's students lambasting the founders for "lack of focus, lack of a great idea, lack of a clear market, lack of just about everything that would earn a passing grade in a business plan class." Then Collins gave his big reveal: "Oh, one more little detail. The names of the founders were Bill Hewlett and David Packard."

The students were stunned. Hewlett and Packard clearly had no competitive advantage, no great product, and no remarkable idea for launching their company. Collins pushed back that they did, indeed, until one of his students finally hit upon this key truth: their great product was the Hewlett-Packard Company itself, and their remarkable idea was the HP Way.

Collins, in his foreword to David Packard's book *The HP Way*, describes the HP Way as "the personal core values of Bill Hewlett and David Packard, and the translation of those values into a comprehensive set of operating practices, cultural norms, and business strategies. The point is not that every company should necessarily adopt the specifics of the HP Way, but that Hewlett and Packard exemplify the power of building a company based on a framework of principles."

The students in that entrepreneurship class left with an understanding that they had never encountered in all of their time at business school. The greatest resource they could offer the world—and the most important foundation upon which to build their various enterprises—was not their product, their services, or even their ideas. It was their values.

CHAPTER SEVEN:
Your Great Ideas Will Die,
Unless . . .

AMPLIFY YOUR LEADERSHIP AS YOU
CONVEY YOUR CORE VALUES

"It was character that got us out of bed, commitment that moved us into action, and discipline that enabled us to follow through."

ZIG ZIGLAR

T here have been plenty of epic failures in company communications, both internal and external, but rather than taking aim at one of these unfortunate organizations, here is an (untrue) urban legend that you may have heard that illustrates a key point.

As the story goes, General Motors made a disastrous mistake when it attempted to introduce the Chevrolet Nova in South America. The model name worked well in the United States, so upper management figured the same name could be used in these countries south of the border. They could not figure out why no one wanted to buy it there, until finally someone realized that, in Spanish, the car's name translated to "No-Go."

As Paul Newman famously quipped in *Cool Hand Luke*, "What we've got here is failure to communicate."

The success of any new idea or initiative depends on far more than the effectiveness of the idea or initiative itself. Your new endeavor may rise or fall depending on communication and its consequences—on how it is presented to your team, how they receive it, and how you and your organization follow up and carry it forward. This chapter presents proven strategies for ensuring that your next major idea or initiative—in this case, the company-wide rollout of your core values—receives the strong start it deserves.

CORE VALUES: THE INTRODUCTION PROCESS
Four Steps to Prepare Your Core Values for Maximum Impact

Leaders are communicators. If you don't communicate well, chances are you won't lead well. One of the most important messages I've ever communicated to my team is our core values. As the leader, I knew I had to get this right.

Once you discover who you are, you too can position your core values for maximum impact in four steps, all revolving around communication.

1. Inform Your Inner Circle

At our leadership team's usual weekly off-site lunch, I was so excited to share my discovery. During lunch, I shared the following:

- My sixteen-year journey and, specifically, my two-and-a-half-year process of discovering my personal values.

- What we had learned about core values in book reviews of Jim Collins's books *Good to Great* and *Built to Last*.

- My six values that described "who I am."

- Where each value came from and why each was important to me.

- My request to *not* reveal the six values to anyone so I could introduce them at an upcoming company-wide meeting.

- My request for them to think over these six values for further discussion at next week's leadership-team lunch.

I was even more energized leaving that lunch because our leadership team was also so excited.

Similarly, you should identify the first people you will contact and share your core values with. Pick those in your trusted, inner circle, but make clear that the values are not to be shared with others until they can be shared with the entire company. Consider giving them time to think over the values and follow up with them at an upcoming meeting in the near future.

2. Infuse Action into Your Core Values

In the following weeks, a couple of interesting things began to unfold. Members of the leadership team took the responsibility of putting "action" words to "Our Values" and came up with:

- *Pursue* Personal Growth.

- *Live* with Integrity.

- *Add* Value to Others.

- *Strive* for Excellence.

- *Enhance* Relationships as We *Drive* for Results.

- *Achieve* Significance.

Take a look at your core values, and consider how you can likewise add words to turn values into actions. This will begin to help you and your team to internalize these values as more than mere tenets—to view them as values intimately connected to actionable long-term goals and to daily decisions and behaviors.

3. Initiate a Logo Design

I hired a graphic design firm to help me with a logo design so I could have it put on a T-shirt for our upcoming QIC-Day, an annual, half-day, company-wide meeting. (QIC is pronounced "Quick" and stands for Quality is Contagious, an internal quality initiative.) I provided the design firm with the key words for our six values—Growth, Integrity, Value, Excellence, Relationships, and Significance—and a few weeks later received a logo design that spelled the word GIVERS. I had not realized what acronym the words spelled!

Your core values may not easily form an acronym, but initiate a logo design that provides a memorable reminder of your values. The simpler and more clearly connected to your core values the logo is, the easier it will be for your people to remember those values. Make this logo an integral part of the rollout of your core values, and take the time to have it done right.

4. Define a Values Statement

You may find that you can benefit from a short statement that encapsulates the essence of your core values. I call this a Values Statement. You can think of a Values Statement as a verbal logo—a simple mantra that relates to *your* core values, providing an easy way for you to champion "who you are" and for your people to remember it! As with the core values, this statement should be unique to your organization. It should not be convoluted; nor should it simply list your core values in a lengthy sentence. By contrast, it should be a brief, memorable phrase that will provide another tool for reinforcing the core values. My company's Values Statement was "People, People, People," and our people knew and understood what it meant: that all of our core values had to do with people, and that without people, none of these values mattered.

Pause for Reflection:

1. *Do your core values include action words?*

2. *Have you initiated a clearly applicable, memorable logo design?*

3. *Does your company have a defined Values Statement?*

How to Roll Out Your Core Values to Your Entire Company

Think about the last organization-wide event that you attended. Did it roll out without a hitch? Was everyone in the room inspired, informed, and aligned? I have hosted countless such meetings and know it's harder than it looks to pull off an event like this.

I advise you to roll out your core values at a company-wide event, as this is a change that affects every person in the company. Also, this type of event can bring everyone onboard with enthusiasm and buy-in. With everything that is riding on your core values, it's important that your event is pulled off successfully, so let's spend a bit of time considering how that can be accomplished.

The secret to these successful meetings cannot be found at the event itself. It occurs long before the first person thumps the microphone and clears his throat to speak!

Preparation

Great leaders spend much more time in the planning of an event than in the event itself.

It is the process of preparing for a well-planned event that makes it successful. When planning an event, the most important questions to begin with are who, what, when, where, how, and why. When you roll out your core values, you can use these important questions to guide the scope, approach, purpose, and content of the event. When you do, it will be a focused team-building experience with lots of fun, fellowship, food, and learning.

Every leader can have a successful company-wide event by addressing five main planning areas:

1. Build Your Event Team

Because the core values rollout is so important to your organization, consider personally asking people to sign up for certain tasks associated with the event.

Your objective should be to ask people on the front lines, those who work with customers and suppliers, to be the answer to your fundamental question of "Who?" so they have some "skin in the game." These assigned roles generate greater anticipation for the upcoming event. Also, when people are involved early, they tend to talk up the upcoming event with their coworkers.

2. Plan the Logistics

This is the basic stuff, without which you can't pull off any event, regardless of its effectiveness! We're talking about a detailed agenda, pens, markers, computer, projector, and handouts. Upbeat instrumental music can be played at the beginning and during refreshment breaks to help warm people up and to increase a high level of anticipation. Position the tables for clear views and small-group interaction, and provide food to encourage prompt arrival, energy to get through the day, and the feeling of a family team.

Observation: The perceived value of a company-provided meal for employees is very high compared with the cost.

3. Plan to Communicate

Notify your key customers and suppliers in advance that you are holding a company-wide event so you can better serve them. This is a great way to manage expectations and emphasize how seriously you value your people and other stakeholders.

You should also think about your seating configuration well in advance and be intentional about who sits where. Print each person's table number on that person's preprinted name tag, which will encourage personal communication during the event.

Tip: Your seating plan can help you build and strengthen your team. You can facilitate new relationships by seating people from different departments or areas at the same table.

Other communication efforts include internal teaser notices you can send in advance of the event—which will increase people's anticipation—and distributed items like T-shirts with the new logo, which your employees can wear to the event. With our rollout, employees saw the GIVERS logo on their new T-shirts but did not yet know what it meant.

4. Plan to Capture

Whether you recruit a photographer or utilize someone in your company, have pictures taken of employees throughout the event so you can post them afterward. People like to see pictures of themselves being part of something so significant. This raises their sense of recognition and self-esteem.

Tip: Task the photographer to capture virtually every person in at least one photo. (This is not a photo shoot with the CEO!)

You can also capture the event through easels and flip charts positioned at the tables, which create an opportunity for people to voice their ideas on a topic. People feel affirmed when their opinions are recorded in such a visible way. At our QIC-Day event, the content from all the flip charts was summarized and distributed after the event. This reinforced that we were listening to people's comments and considered them important enough to reread, summarize, and distribute to the whole company.

Insight: When people see that you recorded and took note of their comments, they are more willing to continue giving suggestions and ideas to improve the business.

5. Plan to Connect

Don't hesitate to make the event fun! Consider offering door prizes. Even if they are as simple as gift cards or bags of candy, you will be amazed at how excited people get over these prizes.

Tip: Time these giveaways for immediately after a refreshment break in order to get people back to their tables on time.

Games are another great way to get everyone involved. I like to use an icebreaker game at the very beginning to get people moving and to help people get to know each other better. You might also use games in which people have team-building fun while learning something about themselves, about you, and about the company. For our core values rollout, we used a game at each table called Wheel of Values (like the *Wheel of Fortune* game on TV) in which the table that was first to guess the correct phrase (related to our Values Statement or core values) got to spin a game wheel for prizes. Loosen up a bit yourself; at our events, I rang a cowbell to round up people after refreshment breaks or at the conclusion of a table exercise, and I received lots of smiles whenever I rang it. Think about finding your own noisemaker—maybe a gong, bell, or horn. Make it yours, and you'll build some fun into your culture!

Insight: When people are having fun and their mouths are open with laughter, you can throw in some teaching for personal growth, and the teaching goes down really well. They get it.

6. Plan to Validate

Think about possibilities for recognizing participation in the event. For many years, I have personally signed certificates with each employee's name as recognition of that person's completion of a workshop, and I have always been impressed by the fact that most of our employees have all of their certificates posted in their workstations.

Tip: Place a copy of each person's certificate in his or her personnel file for future reference. This reflects the person's involvement and underscores the importance of company-wide training and messaging.

7. Plan to Inform and Inspire

This is perhaps the most important part, and it is directly connected to the purpose of the event: rolling out your core values. Your particular approach to sharing your core values will be as uniquely personal to you as the values themselves, but I will share with you how I did it, and you can use whatever is helpful.

Explanation

After the icebreaker game, I spoke about the purpose of the day and explained that our core values define how to behave as we pursue our company's purpose, vision, objectives, and strategic direction. I went on to describe the history of the *process* I went through to discover "who I was," and I was transparent throughout. People heard stories about me that some had never heard before, including some going all the way back to when I was a little boy.

Self-Discovery

I had not yet revealed our core values because I wanted our people to discover them one by one throughout the remainder of the morning.

Tip: Use games and questions to stimulate your people's thinking and discovery. This enables them to connect with the content on a deeper level.

We introduced each value in a similar way. Each table competed to discover each value by playing the Wheel of Values; I shared the meaning of that value, its origin, and its importance to me; and each table then went to a flip chart to discuss and record how we, as a company, were going to live out that value. We wrapped up by having each table report what they discussed, and this process was repeated until every value was discovered.

Distribute Ownership

When we finished the discovery process of our core values, I revealed the connection between the core values and the acronym on their "GIVERS" T-shirts. Next, I introduced Value Leaders who would take *one* value each and form Value Teams to do a deeper dive into how we, as a company, were going to "live out" that value.

Observation: When you place others in leadership positions, they dig deeper, grow more, and produce better results than if you tried to do all the "leading" yourself.

Clarify Outcomes

Near the end, we had two more discussion questions addressed at the flip charts, followed by reporting from each table. The two questions were: As an organization . . .

- If we *fail* to align our behaviors/activities with our core values, what will the outcomes be?

- If we *succeed* at aligning our behaviors/activities with our core values, what will the outcomes be?

Remind the Team

In closing, I made some final remarks, and we showed a slideshow with pictures of just about every employee being involved in past events, which emphasized the importance of people—the underlying factor in all our core values. And I shared about the "Our Values" plaque that would soon be unveiled in our office foyer.

Action Plans

We wrapped up the core values QIC-Day by having people prepare their Personal Action Plans handout as to what action steps they needed to take to align with our core values. Then all the employees placed their plans inside a sealed, self-addressed envelope to themselves. We mailed the envelopes by the end of December, when people are considering their New Year's resolutions, as a timely reminder of their Personal Action Plans.

Celebrate!

The QIC-Day ended with a catered celebration lunch. The room was filled with laughter and conversation about people's lives, the business, *and* our newly announced core values!

Insight: As leaders, we're often focused on results and are anxious to "check off" a task or event and get on with our business. Take time to celebrate big wins or important events. Celebration helps keep everyone energized and passionate about all aspects of the business.

As you can see, it takes a lot of planning and preparation to effectively roll out your core values to your team. But considering how important it is to your success, it is worth all the effort!

I hope these techniques are useful to you as you invest time, energy, and thought into planning the rollout of your core values with your organization. This is one of the most important messages you will ever communicate, so the investment you make now will reap tremendous dividends in the future.

Pause for Reflection:

1. *How much time do you usually take to prepare for a company-wide meeting?*

2. *Which of the above ideas are you going to implement for your next event?*

CORE VALUES: THE FOLLOW-UP
Expand the Impact of Your Next Event

Have you ever attended a conference, workshop, or meeting that just blew your socks off? You walked away enthused, pumped, and ready to go and take on the world!

How often have you heard great ideas and felt highly encouraged by what was said—but *never* heard any more talk or discussion about those ideas after you walked away? It's as if the "head of steam" that developed during the event dissipated in the silence that followed.

You want to be intentional and careful to prevent this from happening with the rollout of your company's core values.

Check It Off

Oftentimes, leaders roll out their ideas or new initiatives at a meeting or conference, and before the stage lights dim, they check off the event as "done" on their to-do list.

As leaders, when we hastily check off an important event and race off to the next item on our lists, we miss an opportunity to reinforce the main objectives of the event. However, *every leader can increase the long-term effectiveness of an event by engaging the organization's people in post event leadership assignments.*

This is of great value and importance when considering how to share and implement company-wide core values. Of course, the following strategies can also be effectively utilized for any other new idea or initiative that you want to take root and grow rather than wither away.

Tap Your Inner Circle

When you roll out key initiatives such as core values, get your executive team or inner circle in on the action. Long before the event, ask them to recommend which employees could become ambassadors for these new initiatives. This process gets your inner circle thinking about the initiatives in a deeper way and helps them focus on other people in your organization who could help reinforce your key ideas or initiatives.

Ask for Commitment

We called these employees who exemplified one of our core values our "Value Leaders." Before the event, go to each of the designated people and ask if they will perform a special role in the upcoming company-wide event.

Note: I did not reveal what their role would be, because I wanted them to experience the powerful process of discovering our core values with the rest of the company during the event.

Cast the Vision

Follow up with your Value Leaders and cast the vision for them. Immediately after our QIC-Day, I met with our Value Leaders and thanked them for agreeing to this very important leadership role. I told them they had been uniquely selected by the executive team because we had already observed their personal commitment to one of these values that were critical to the foundation of everything our company was built on. We did not want to just talk about our core values, I shared with them; we wanted them lived out.

Expand the Team

These leaders are not only good examples of their assigned core value but can also perform significant leadership roles. Consider asking each Value Leader to choose a team of three to five like-minded people who have lived out the one value assigned to that leader. This allows more people to get in on the discovery, learning, and reinforcement of your core values.

Define the Task

An important aspect of leadership is defining what you expect your people to do and deliver. Take the time to explain what you expect of your newly appointed Value Leaders. For example, you can:

- Task every Value Team to study your company's current behaviors and find any gaps between what is said and what is actually done. Plus, you can ask them to develop ideas for how the organization might further its efforts regarding each value.

- Suggest they use the flip charts from the company-wide event as a starting point to do a deeper dive into how the company is going to live out that value.

- Ask them to present their recommendations at a second company-wide event, which you can schedule for the following month or whenever makes the most sense.

Notice that it only requires simple steps to create widespread collaboration and support of your core values.

Pause for Reflection:

1. *Have you ever been frustrated with the lack of follow-through from your team after an important meeting or event?*

2. *In what way(s) could you, as the leader, change your approach and increase the post event follow-through of your team?*

3. *How do you involve your employees in the follow-up and follow-through after an organization-wide event?*

Make Your Core Values Stick

After our QIC-Day, I gave the new Value Leaders a one-month deadline to report at our next company-wide QIC-Day. I was amazed how quickly they moved forward in their new roles. As soon as I stepped away, the Value Leaders had their own stand-up meeting.

Tip: Stand-up meetings are a good tool
for the leader's toolbox. Stand-ups
encourage people to quickly:

- Determine the main objectives.
- Define the priorities.
- Decide on next actions to move forward.

It was fun to overhear the Value Leaders talk about the selection process for their Value Teams. You would have thought this was the official NFL draft by the way they were trading team members between themselves.

Core Values Follow-Up Event

At a follow-up event one month later (a half-day QIC-Day), we encouraged everyone to wear their GIVERS T-shirts and used the Wheel of Values game at multiple strategic times to emphasize our company's purpose, vision, and objectives. I also reviewed our core values, using each letter in GIVERS as a springboard for discussing the related value. Starting with the letter "G" for "Pursue Personal **G**rowth," each Value Leader presented the outcomes from their Value Team discussions on how we were and should be living out that value.

Insight: When you let others in your
organization "take the stage" in a leadership
role, you empower them to learn and grow—
and their job satisfaction skyrockets!

I shared comments about each value, and each table discussed and recorded additional thoughts about how we, as a company, were going to live out that value on a daily basis. We used games to reinforce the values and keep the energy level high, and we closed the day by revealing a new plaque in the entryway that displayed our core values for employees, customers, and suppliers to view each day as they entered our building.

Tip: Create visual representations of the most important principles in your company, such as your core values. These don't have to be videos or plaques; they can be as simple as a framed certificate on the wall of your business. These serve as visual reminders to you, your employees, your customers, and your suppliers!

Pause for Reflection:

1. *What's one new way you can reinforce the core values of your organization?*

2. *How could you assign special roles and responsibilities to your people that would encourage them to adopt and champion your core values?*

Lead Better with These Five Follow-Up Strategies

So you've rolled out your core values to your organization, and now you're wondering, "What now?" Whether you are a "mom-and-pop shop" or a large company, any big initiative that you roll out to all your people takes a lot of effort! Here's what to do next.

I've learned that as you wrap up your meeting and turn *off* the lights in the meeting room, it's time to turn *on* your efforts to follow up with your people!

The two QIC-Day meetings—one to introduce our core values and one to follow up through our Value Leaders—were important. But I believe what happened *after* the second meeting was key to our successful core-values rollout.

> # The secret to the success of great leaders is the time they spend on the follow-up and follow-through of an event or a decision.

Every leader can improve his or her leadership by using the following five follow-up strategies.

1. Management By Walking Around (MBWA)

Immediately after each company-wide meeting, try your hand at MB-WA—"Management By Walking Around." Take the time to walk around and talk with your employees. Your goal might be to discover what they learned, what they thought about your core values, and how the company can improve.

When the leader of the organization sincerely spends time talking with a front-line person:

- The leader and employee see each other as real people.
- Relationships are enhanced.
- The front-line person's self-esteem takes a major jump. When employees feel good about themselves, strong results follow.

- The leader gains new insights about the business's customers and learns what is really going on "in the trenches."

2. Thank-Yous

Immediately after each company-wide event, write personal thank-you notes to those who were major contributors to the meeting. As much as possible, go directly to those with other roles and personally thank them.

I've learned that employees appreciate a written or verbal thank-you when they have helped with a special event or meeting. They want to know you appreciate their efforts outside their normal day-to-day responsibilities.

3. Value Leaders

Ask the Value Leaders and their teams to help ensure behaviors continue to be aligned with your core values. You can also ask them to lead the implementation of any ideas that emerge from their team discussions to ensure there are no gaps in behaviors.

Don't underestimate the value of distributed leadership! At my company, the Value Leaders and their teams ended up being the biggest internal cheerleaders of our core values. They kept these values front and center throughout the organization.

4. VIP (Values In Practice)

Look for ways to find and recognize those who are acting out your core values. You can begin continuously looking across the organization to identify people as "VIPs" by catching them putting one of your core values into practice. What gets recognized gets repeated! When you look for ways to affirm living out your core values, people start to understand how to apply the core values to their everyday jobs. Plus, the recognition creates a desire to repeat the desired behavior again and again and again!

5. Inner Circle (Executive Team)

When your inner circle meets following the rollout of your core values, those values need to be among the top topics of your agenda every time. For the values to become meaningful, you need to talk about them at every opportunity.

Propagating your core values to your entire organization starts with the key leaders at the top. If you get them involved in the early stages of the process, your key leaders will become your company-wide champions of a new message or initiative.

I've highlighted five ways to connect with and lead your people. These strategies helped me roll out our core values to our people, and they can help you, too!

Pause for Reflection:

1. *What is one strategy you have used to connect with employees and reinforce the core values of your organization?*

2. *What attributes or actions do you recognize and reward within your organization?*

How to Ensure Your Organization's Core Values Alignment

The Penteconter galley of ancient Greece is considered to be one of the first true warships in history. It was propelled by fifty oars, each powered by a single man. The ship was long and sleek, and the oars were roughly nine feet in length. Sails were held in reserve as a secondary means of moving through the waves—manpower was the preferred method.

During battle, at times the Penteconter was rowed forward at such speed that it was used as a battering ram against other ships. It was of utmost importance that the rowers worked in synergy. To accomplish this, a captain or coxswain would shout out rowing chants or beat a drum, and the rowers would pull their oars in unison. What made this ship so powerful—able to plow right into enemy ships, which could then be boarded and conquered—boiled down to a single factor, without which they would have been literally sunk: every person pulled *together*.

Alignment Defined

The other day, I took my car into the shop to get the oil changed, tires rotated, and wheels aligned. As you may know, failure to correct misalignment of your wheels usually results in uneven tire wear and your vehicle pulling to the left or to the right. This misalignment leads to the expense of frequent tire replacement, driver fatigue, and even danger resulting from the vehicle's inability to hold a straight line when driven. Fix the alignment issues, and many of the present and future problems go away.

Alignment occurs when *all* the elements of an organization work together in concert within the context and boundaries of the organization's *only* sacred cow: Core Ideology = Core Values + Purpose. By "*all* elements," I'm talking about goals, strategies, tactics, policies, processes, cultural practices, management behaviors, building layouts, pay systems, accounting systems, and job design—essentially everything that the organization does.

When your organization is aligned, it is guided first by your own internal compass (which points to what makes perfect sense for and is appropriate for *your* company, however unusual), not by the standards, practices, conventions, forces, trends, fads, fashions, and buzzwords of the outer world. The evidence from the research done by Jim Collins found amazing truths about the good-to-great companies:

- They used a participative leadership style that was reinforced by employees being:

- o   Trained in participative leadership skills.

- o   Involved in the decision-making process.

- They hired people who had the same core values and who strongly lived them out. Consequently, the problems of commitment, alignment, motivation, and change just melted away.

Through my participative leadership style, our employees knew that I was as much working for them as they were for me. This way of leading literally turned our organizational chart upside down! When you accomplish that, you have a *team* of people aligned and all rowing in the same direction.

Every leader can ensure organizational alignment by following a two-step process.

1. Identify and Correct Misalignments

The first step is an analytic process that requires the discipline of the organization to uncover and eliminate any misalignments promoting behavior that:

- Is inconsistent with or drives people away from the organization's core values.

- Impedes or blocks progress.

Insight: Employees pick up on all the signals in their work environment—big and small—as cues for how they should behave. They are ever watchful for the tiny inconsistencies. You do *not* want employees to say, "See, there you go. I knew management was just blowing smoke. They don't really believe their own rhetoric."

One way to allow your organization to quickly identify misalignment without pointing fingers is to put random people into groups of no more than six and ask each group to come up with the three most significant misalignments pertaining to each core value. Typically, each group will identify the same misalignments.

Example: If you say teamwork is a core value, but you compensate people on individual performance, you've got to change your compensation structure.

2. Create New Alignment

The second step is a creative process requiring the invention of new mechanisms, processes, and strategies to bring the core values to life and to stimulate progress. This process involves a variety of strategies, including visual reminders, communication tactics, and changes to the ways you hire, orient, and evaluate employees.

Visuals

Visual reminders are a powerful method of communicating and reinforcing your message to your organization. They keep your message top-of-mind for your team members.

I was open to every kind of approach to visually reminding us all of our core values, including the T-shirts, the entryway plaque, payroll stuffers that highlighted our core values, and desk displays.

Insight: As leaders, we tend to think, "I said it once, so let us get back to work." What I've learned is that we all need constant and consistent reminders as to "who we are" as an organization, as do our customers and suppliers. The message never changes, but the method is always changing.

Human Resources

In Jim Collins's books *Good to Great* and *Built to Last,* the evidence from his research revealed that the organizations with the greatest financial results were the organizations whose employees shared the same values. And they were like fanatics about the values.

The best way to build a high-performance, values-aligned team is to hire people who share your values.

Hiring Interviews: We changed our interview process and started asking the candidates more high-quality discovery questions. This helped us ensure that the prospective employees' values were aligned with ours. There are two general types of questions:

- *"What* questions" concern facts, such as, "What was your first job after you graduated from college?"

- *"How* and *Why* questions" can provide insights into the other person's goals, plans, priorities, principles, *values,* behaviors, and ethics. These are questions like, "Why did you leave your last job?"

The *what* questions and the answers to them are important. But one of the most useful and important aspects of the *what* questions is the fact that they open the door for the *how* and *why* questions. And it's the answers to these questions that provide you the opportunity to hear how the other person thinks. The importance of assessing a potential employee's goals, *values*, priorities, and behaviors can't be overemphasized!

Insight: Learn to wait to hire the right person even when you need someone quickly. In our company, we had a saying: "When in doubt, leave them out."

New Employee Indoctrination/Orientation: We went to great lengths at the very beginning to ensure that new employees understood "who we were" and how we wanted them to behave.

Insight: When you hire the "right" people with the same values, you do not need a bureaucracy to manage them. But you do manage the systems that the "right" people use to perform their work.

Employee Evaluations: Even though we should evaluate employees' performance daily, our annual formal evaluations included how well our employees were living out our core values. When your people understand that part of their performance will be evaluated against how they align with the company's values, they become more intentional about exhibiting those values.

What gets inspected gets done.

Business Meetings: Meetings provide another way to reinforce your message and check for alignment. When we are face to face with our team, we have a unique opportunity to emphasize what is important and echo our core values to our people.

Friday Stand-Ups: These were very short weekly meetings with all employees present. This was a great time to update people about what was going on in the company and to emphasize and reinforce our core values.

Business Reviews: During these monthly financial and operating reports meetings, I would often comment about how a situation tied back to our core values or how the behavior of an employee exemplified those values.

State of the Company: Three times a year, we would gather everyone together to communicate the "state of the company." I would always begin these meetings with a review of our core values.

Every leader can use visual reminders, human resource practices, and business meetings to reinforce key messages to his or her people. Remember: you never attain absolute alignment. But you can make meaningful progress toward alignment if you work at it consistently over time. It's not just the big pieces but also the itty-bitty details that make a big impression. Together, big and small efforts combine to create an overall effect that leads to enduring greatness.

Pause for Reflection:

1. *How's your company performing?*
2. *Is it time for a core-values alignment?*
3. *What progress are you making on eliminating your misalignments?*

PART V
WORKPLACE CULTURE

CHAPTER EIGHT:
Great Leaders Don't Focus on Culture

FOCUS YOUR LEADERSHIP ON THE FUNDAMENTALS, AND THE RIGHT CULTURE WILL FOLLOW

"Culture is the consequence of the values by which we live."

CHARLES DAY

There is a reason that the important topic of culture is placed at this particular point in the book. In life (and within this book), everything that has gone before has prepared us for where we are now. Much like how we stand on the shoulders of those who have gone before us, this section on culture is only fully realized if we understand, embrace, and apply the principles that precede it.

Perhaps I can explain it this way. The principles of relationships and results, process and content, principle over expedience, and core values all lay a foundation that is essential to extraordinary workplace culture. Yet while it is good for us to desire and work toward healthy and dynamic workplace cultures, it should not be our primary aim!

"What?" you say. "I thought this was a book about workplace culture! If we desire the best culture possible, shouldn't that be our main focus?"

I have learned that to achieve meaningful culture change, you need to focus on the fundamentals that support the culture you desire. Culture, then, is the fruit, not the goal!

Culture is the fruit, not the goal!

Question: If culture is better described as an end result rather than the main object of our attention, what should we focus on?

Answer: Our primary focus must be on the foundational elements of our organization—our core values, purpose, and vision, as well as how we lead our team. Once you identify these elements, clearly communicate them, and incorporate them into your behavior, the culture that you so desire will emerge before your very eyes!

Merely rolling a ping-pong table into the break room and providing free sodas for all will not produce the vibrant, engaged workplace that you want. While those are fine things, providing such perks without the meaningful context created through values-driven leadership will mean that they ultimately fall short of their intended purpose!

As we walk through the coming pages on the various facets of outstanding cultures, you'll see plenty of opportunities to employ the principles of leading and managing, process and content, principle over expedience, and an abundance mindset versus a scarcity mindset. And it all starts with the leader.

Leaders Define Their Culture

Every organization has a culture, be it good or bad. And be it good or bad, your culture is always driven by the leader—the owner, president, CEO, general manager, or department head. So if you want to improve your culture, you, as the leader, must champion the improvements.

You may be asking right now, "Won't we need to back off from driving for the results we need in order to improve our culture?" The answer is absolutely *no*. I would suggest you continue to drive for results and keep high expectations *while* adding improvements to your culture, which is the "people side" of your business.

Unexpected Outcomes

Some principles are hidden below the surface of the common and expected practices of business. Their power goes untapped because it takes some faith to put these principles into action. Employing values-driven leadership to build and strengthen your culture is one of these principles. You'll find that as you focus on the fundamentals (like participative leadership) and center your business around your core values, you'll create a great culture where your people will be inspired to help you achieve the results you want.

At our company, we definitely were not perfect, but we got more intentional about our core values and how we led our people over time. The result was an inspiring culture. From 2005 through 2011, our company experienced significant growth during tough economic times when many other companies were declining. As I mentioned before, our revenue and profit both grew about five times, and we were twice named in the 100 Best Companies to Work for in Texas list. And just as importantly, we created a workplace where people enjoyed being a part of our team.

Culture is as important as (if not more important than) your business strategy because it either strengthens or undermines your business and the objectives you are trying to achieve. Step back, define, and evaluate your workplace culture—both what it is now and what you want it to be in the future.

This process of improving your workplace culture is not a sprint; it takes time and intentional leadership. As you begin to survey your culture and look for areas to enhance, I encourage you to identify one aspect of your workplace culture that you would like to improve and then focus on that one area.

I suggest you periodically rate your progress in the various aspects of your workplace culture. Such analysis can help you refine your efforts. Plus, it's an effective way to assess the strength of your leadership and your defining values and principles.

A farmer plants, tends, prunes, cultivates, and grows the *trees*, not the *fruit*—the fruit is the result of the farmer's labors. Remember: culture is the fruit, not the goal!

Pause for Reflection:

1. *Would you like to improve the performance of your organization?*

2. *Have you considered the importance of employing a values-driven leadership approach when seeking to improve your workplace culture?*

Three Leadership Practices That Will Stunt Your Team's Growth

I asked you an important question before: Do you have *individuals* on a team or a team of individuals? As Michael Jordan said: "Talent wins games, but teamwork and intelligence wins championships." As good as he was, he couldn't win the games all by himself. It took a team working together to achieve those results time and time again.

Talent wins games, but teamwork and intelligence wins championships.

—MICHAEL JORDAN

All organizations want to be great. So what keeps good organizations from becoming great? Why don't they win championships? The answer is found in the leadership of the organization. Most leaders focus on *good* things, but they could create great organizations by focusing on the *right* things.

Good is the enemy of great.

—JIM COLLINS

You may say, "I'm fighting hard every day to make it work, and it's still not working. What am I missing?" Often, leaders do and say things that destroy the spirit of *team*work. Consequently, they limit the success of the whole organization.

Every leader can build a dynamic team by avoiding three common leadership practices.

1. Emphasizing Event over Process

Leaders tend to implement big, grand programs, have "great" ideas, make radical changes, and chronically restructure, always looking for the one killer innovation, lucky break, or miracle moment. In doing so, they skip the necessary emphasis on process and the corporate habits that lay the foundation for success.

By neglecting the power of sustained, incremental process, leaders bounce from event to event and fail to map out a consistent roadmap for progress.

2. Using Fear to Influence Behavior

Leaders often threaten their people, using fear to obtain compliance to policies or initiatives. Whether directly stated or implied, they leverage uncertainty in an effort to control and direct their employees' actions. Sometimes, leaders even play on the fear of being left behind in the marketplace in an attempt to encourage innovation and competitiveness.

Fear limits the potential of all concerned. It serves to demotivate and discourage folks, and it chokes off their drive and initiative.

3. Demonstrating Chronic Inconsistency

Leaders often push organizations in one direction, then stop, change course, and throw them in new directions. And then they stop, change course, and throw them into yet other directions. After years of lurching back and forth, they fail to build and sustain momentum. This behavior leaves people unsure of the direction and even the purpose of the organization.

Is your team winning championships? If not, could it be that your behavior as a leader is stifling true *team*work and limiting the success of your organization? Ask yourself: *Do you have* individuals *on your team, or are you a* team *of individuals?*

Great leaders build great cultures in which their teams win and profits soar. Let's explore workplace culture and its importance to your success!

Pause for Reflection:

1. *Do you value events or incremental, sustained process?*

2. *Do you rely on the use of fear when leading your team?*

What Is Culture, Anyway?

It's become a buzzword in the last few years. We all have our own ideas of what it is and what it isn't. But what is culture, really? Zappos's CEO, Tony Hsieh, expresses the importance of culture by stating, "Your brand is your culture." For the stressed-out leader, Hsieh also provides unconventional advice when he explains, "If you get the culture right, most of the other stuff will just take care of itself." Merriam-Webster defines culture as "the beliefs, customs, arts, etc., of a particular society, group, place, or time . . . a way of thinking, behaving, or working that exists in a place or organization (such as a business)."[3] Employers Resource Council, a human-resources organization, describes it this way:

> Culture is the character and personality of an organization. It's the sum of the core values, beliefs, traditions, underlying assumptions, attitudes, and behaviors shared by a group of people. Stated simply, culture is what makes your organization unique.[4]

If culture is so fundamental, why is it so hard to define? Culture is like the wind. It's difficult to describe, but you can see the manifestations or effects of culture in action.

I have always viewed core values as driving culture and culture as a manifestation of a business's core values. In fact, if you take a careful look around your organization, you will see visible signs of its culture and the core values that drive it.

What Does Culture Look Like?

Though core values are intangible, the culture they drive is observable. It

---

[3] *Merriam-Webster's Learner's Dictionary*, s.v. "culture," www.learnersdictionary.com/definition/culture.

[4] Employers Resource Council, "Workplace Culture: What It Is, Why It Matters, & How to Define It," *HR Insights Blog*, March 6, 2013, https://www.yourerc.com/blog/post/Workplace-Culture-What-it-Is-Why-it-Matters-How-to-Define-It.aspx.

manifests itself through your people's behavior as they pursue the organization's purpose, vision, objective(s), strategies, tactics, and performance goals.

The visual and verbal components of an organization's culture are noticeable every day at work. Whether you are walking through a work area, sitting in an office, attending a meeting, or eating in the lunchroom, the organization's culture surrounds you and permeates your working life.

What Shapes Workplace Culture?

Culture starts at the top! In addition to being particularly influenced by the organization's founder, culture is also influenced by the executives and other managerial staff because of their roles in decision making and strategic direction. As a leader, you have a great opportunity to intentionally influence the culture of your organization.

People do what people see. I found in my own business that our people behaved as I did and sought out what I thought was important. They would use language like I did, and, being from Texas, sometimes that wasn't a good thing! In fact, I would often say we were going to hand out Texas Dictionaries so people could understand me.

For better or for worse, I knew that I set the example, and I never took that responsibility lightly. I also continued to look for new ways to enhance our culture so we didn't become stagnant.

You shape culture through:

- *What* you communicate. Do you champion your organization's core values, purpose, vision, and goals? What stories do you and other leaders tell about people in your organization and about company happenings? What do you emphasize, recognize, and celebrate?

- *How* you communicate. Do you exhibit your core values in your personal and workplace behavior? Are you consistent in living them out as you pursue your organization's purpose, vision, and goals?

Take some time today to look around. Walk through your organization, and observe your culture. Listen to what your people are saying. Ask yourself the following questions in order to clarify your understanding of your own culture:

- What do I/they say, and how do I/they say it?

- What do we do, and how do we do it?

- Whom do I employ?

- What does our workplace look like?

Studies suggest a correlation between financial results and a strong, inspiring organizational culture. If you do not thoroughly understand your organization's culture, your organization is probably underperforming, and you're almost certainly missing opportunities to improve results.

You might be amazed to learn all the things in your business that affect and reflect its culture. In fact, all leaders can better understand their culture by observing four main areas in their organization in addition to their own leadership.

1. People, People, People!

I have always said that the three keys to my companies' successes were "people, people, people!" Culture starts with people.

Think about:

- Your hiring process. Where do you look for new team members? How do you evaluate candidates? Do you consider whether their traits, beliefs, and core values align with your organization?

- How you onboard new hires. What kind of training and orientation do they receive? How do you introduce them to your organization and your core values? What steps do you take to ensure that they smoothly and quickly integrate with your team?

- How you treat your people. Are they treated like assets or just as the cost of doing business? What programs do you have in place to serve your people and reinforce your core values?

2. Information Flows

The flow of information in your organization strongly affects its culture. In order to explore this area more deeply, consider the following questions:

- What kind of information is distributed in your company? Is it easy for your people to stay up to date about important information? This could include key metrics on company performance, new opportunities, or challenges.

- How about information regarding your people? Do you highlight employee achievements, accolades, and hobbies? Are major family events like birthdays, births, and upcoming retirements recognized?

- Where does the information flow in your organization? It can flow vertically from one level to another. It also flows horizontally among coworkers.

- What methods and media do you use to communicate with your team? Do you use email or an internal web portal to keep people up to date? How do you use face-to-face meetings to communicate with your people?

3. Policies and Practices

The policies and practices within your organization have their own impact on its culture. Consider how:

- Policies regarding pay scales, benefits, and opportunities to advance within the company all influence and help define your culture.

- Rules related to discipline and dress code also influence the overall culture of the organization.

- Policies and practices that govern how you do business, how you interact with suppliers, and how you serve customers all help to shape your organizational culture.

4. Facilities, Inside and Out

The physical appearance of the inside and outside of an organization's place of business speaks volumes about the organization's culture. Walk around your place of business, and observe how the following items shape your culture:

- Things that your company displays or exhibits.

- Personal touches that people bring to the workplace.

- The layout and organization of workspaces and common areas.

- Cleanliness and orderliness of the inside and outside of the facility, how sound and noise are controlled, and the general upkeep of premises.

In our company, we strategically used our walls to reinforce the foundational aspect of teamwork. On some walls, we had pictures of all our employees in front of a group of our trucks. Other walls displayed our employees in front of our facilities. We even had a photo of our employees

186 | PRINCIPLED PROFITS

standing on the bridge in front of our city's signature waterfalls. Each photo was attractively matted, framed, and signed by each of the employees in the company. Because I'm a bicycling enthusiast, our people gave me a special gift of a framed Albert cycling jersey surrounded by the signatures of every employee, which I displayed with pride. We also used our walls to showcase framed versions of our past marketing materials, which we used to explain the history of our company.

The culture of your organization is affected by your people, information flows, policies and practices, and workplace environment. Your leadership determines the direction of all of these factors. The good news is that as you become aware of any deficiencies in your culture, you can take active steps to lead your people toward the culture you desire!

Pause for Reflection:

1. *How much time do you spend thinking about and intentionally influencing your organization's culture?*

2. *What one area of your organizational culture will you examine today?*

Four Benefits of an Inspired Workplace Culture

People, processes, and profits (among a host of other things) vie for a leader's time and attention. And most leaders have difficulty determining what's most important.

During my early years of leadership, I focused on:

- Strategies.
- Innovation in service offerings.
- Optimization of operations.

You see, I was going after predictability and results. I was focused on strategy.

Our people were always important in our business. But it was not until 1989 that I got intentional about our people. And when I started focusing on our people, over and above any policy, system, or strategy, I began to learn what management guru Peter Drucker already knew: "Culture eats strategy for breakfast."

I began to understand that if I had a culture that focused on our people, they would help me pursue and achieve the financial results I was looking for. When I began to have our people participate in decisions, created a family atmosphere, and helped develop them, they gave back in ways above and beyond what I anticipated. They responded with loyalty, mutual trust, teamwork, and commitment.

You can appropriately focus on culture by understanding the following benefits of an inspired organizational culture:

- *An inspired organizational culture attracts high-performing people (and keeps them)*. A strong, positive culture can be your best form of marketing. Top performers gravitate to organizations where they can contribute and feel appreciated. A strong culture broadcasts a message of opportunity to best-in-field people.

- *An inspired organizational culture creates a united team*. An inspired workplace culture draws your people together in pursuit of common goals and outcomes. This creates a cohesiveness and unity that enables your team to effectively respond to difficulties and capitalize on new opportunities.

- *An inspired organizational culture increases employees' sense of well-being*. Research by Deloitte links a strong workplace culture to employee happiness and satisfaction. Employees feel happier when they have similar core values and share a strong sense of purpose with their coworkers.

- *An inspired organizational culture boosts financial performance.* Several studies (including one conducted by Booz & Company and the Bertelsmann Foundation in 2004) indicate a correlation between financial results and a strong, inspiring organizational culture. Jon Katzenbach with Booz & Company states: "Culture can become a 'secret weapon' that makes extraordinary things happen."

The benefits of strong cultures are clear. Most companies' cultures develop over time through happenstance instead of through intentional decisions filtered through the core values of the organization. But you can begin to be intentional about your culture today by asking the following questions:

- Do you consistently attract best-in-class talent?

- What is your turnover rate? How does it compare with the best organizations in your industry?

- Do your people enjoy their jobs and workplace? How do you know?

- Is your company in the top tier of performance, efficiency, and profit in your market segment?

Pause for Reflection:

1. *How do your answers to these questions help you understand your current culture?*

2. *Have you ever asked your people how well they enjoy their jobs?*

How to Win in the Marketplace

I have learned that the best way to excel in the marketplace is to first excel in your workplace. So how do you excel in the workplace? You create an excellent, or "winning," culture.

Employers Resource Council (ERC), a human-resources organization based in Northeastern Ohio, has run an annual program for over fifteen years that "recognizes great workplaces that excel at the attraction, retention, and motivation of top performers" and has identified fifteen attributes that it believes "are characteristic of great workplaces for top talent."[5]

Let's look at the ERC's attributes of a winning culture. Every leader can help cultivate a great workplace by developing the following attributes in his or her culture.

Meaningful and Challenging Work

Think back over the many projects you have undertaken, and reflect on which of them were the most satisfying to you when completed. When has your work been the most compelling, and when have you felt the most driven to accomplish it? Odds are, you're not thinking of times when the work was simple and easy, and you coasted by with minimal effort.

The first attribute I'd like to highlight from ERC's findings describes employees' work:

> It [the "great workplace" employer] understands the importance of keeping employees' work interesting, exciting, challenging and meaningful, because consistently, top performers say that challenging and meaningful work is the number one attribute they seek in a job.[6]

---

[5] Employers Resource Council, "The 15 Attributes of a Great Workplace," *HR Insights Blog*, September 5, 2013, https://www.yourerc.com/blog/post/The-15-Attributes-of-a-Great-Workplace.aspx.

[6] Ibid.

Over the years, I have experienced that our people in our company wanted huge and daunting goals that were bigger than themselves. These goals were like mountains to climb whose lofty heights on the horizon inspired and motivated our team in their daily work as they advanced toward the peaks. After all, there is something about gazing upon a towering summit that inspires us in a way that a nearby hilltop simply does not.

As the key leader, it was my responsibility to put these goals before our people and explain why they were important. Because I also learned to involve the right people in the decision-making process, I could ensure from the beginning that the work would be meaningful and challenging to them.

Competitive Compensation Plus Incentive Pay

Although employees are driven by a desire for meaningful and challenging work and all of us would like to contribute to society, let's face it: everybody likes to get paid. As Zig Ziglar put it, "Money isn't the most important thing in life, but it's reasonably close to oxygen on the 'Gotta have it' scale."

The second attribute I'd like to explore from ERC's findings addresses employees' compensation and incentives:

> It [the "great workplace" employer] offers competitive and fair compensation, above-average pay increases, and opportunities to earn more pay based on performance, such as bonuses, profit sharing, and other incentives to keep and reward top performing talent as well as attract new talent.[7]

Prior to hiring a professional organization to prepare a wage survey of each position, our company used whatever outside source we could find to determine a wage range for each position. Our first objective was to ensure we were paying a fair wage for each position.

---

[7] Ibid.

We then set up a Pay for Performance incentive/bonus for all employees. We paid out a percentage of the profits to our people when our profits exceeded a certain threshold. Each month, we shared our progress toward the threshold. At that time, we paid out annually, and our people received some the largest bonus checks they had ever seen.

One year, we came very close to the threshold, but we did not go over it. However, as the owner, I still gave our people the bonus because I knew in my heart they had given their best. It was very exciting to see people's faces when we gave out the bonus checks. One lady came by my office and gave me a big bear hug. It was obvious that sharing our profits helped endear folks to me and our company. It also boosted productivity, increased satisfaction, and helped retention.

Pause for Reflection:

1. *Do you provide challenging and meaningful work to your people? What would your top performers say if you asked them?*

2. *Have you surveyed your industry to assess if your pay scales and incentive pay are competitive?*

Listen and Collaborate

Here's a truth I have discovered to be particularly powerful: people will follow a worthy leader before they will follow a worthy cause.

Consider William Wallace, who was a Scottish knight and one of Scotland's greatest national heroes. The Scottish, oppressed by an English king who had jailed their own king and declared himself ruler of Scotland, already had a worthy cause. But Wallace spearheaded his country's charge to restore its independence and freedom, and armies rallied behind him. His influence even carried on after his death, as his martyrdom fueled the fires of independence—finally won more than two decades after his execution. The Scottish armies were fighting for their homeland, but they were following Wallace.

While you are not likely to wield a sword in the office, there are other ways to earn the respect and loyalty of those who look to you for direction. The next attribute from the ERC report describes some of the powerful outcomes of participatory leadership:

> Great workplaces involve and empower employees by listening to their input, involving them in moving the organization forward, and giving them opportunities to lead initiatives, collaborate with one another, participate in decision-making, and make a meaningful difference at work. At great workplaces, employees believe that their opinions matter and that they can positively impact their organizations.[8]

As a leader, I discovered there is more power in asking questions than barking orders. In our company, we had an organizational teaching called **AQL**, which stood for *"Ask Questions and Listen."* We went to great lengths to learn how to ask good, quality discovery questions, not only of ourselves but also of our customers and suppliers.

As we've discussed, I also developed ways to involve the right people in the decision-making process. When people understand that you depend on their opinions and guidance to make better decisions, they become team members who give their very best for the success of the organization.

If you are worried that such participatory leadership will lessen your position of power, understand that listening to others and collaborating with them does not reduce your authority—it enhances it. As you show yourself willing to involve others in key decisions and participate with them in the joint venture of your organization, they will respond in kind with greater willingness to follow your lead.

---

[8] Ibid.

Genuine Care and Mutual Respect Leads to Trust

Did you ever play Monopoly as a kid and wish that all of that fake money was real currency? Well, you're not alone in your desire for quick cash; according to the Secret Service, there is nearly $9 million in counterfeit money circulating in the United States. Despite sophisticated efforts by counterfeiters, though, trained individuals—looking for everything from watermarks to color-shifting ink—can easily spot a fake.

In the same way, your employees will be able to tell from a mile away whether your leadership is based on genuine care and authentic trust or whether it is, in a word, fake.

The ERC reports:

Great workplaces are led by exceptional and inspiring leaders. Leaders set the example from the top and lead the organization well. They genuinely care about and value employees. Relationships between leaders and employees are characterized by mutual respect, trust, honesty, and support.[9]

I learned that trust was the glue that held our organization together and allowed me to influence our people. If I broke our people's trust, I could no longer influence them. People will forgive occasional mistakes when they know you, as the leader, are bigger on the inside than you are on the outside. But when you break trust, you forfeit your ability to lead, and you can no longer expect to keep influencing your people.

Leaders earn respect and trust by:

- Integrity: Making sound decisions.
- Humility: Admitting your mistakes.
- Authenticity: Being yourself with everyone.

---

[9] Ibid.

- Sincerity: Putting what's best for your followers and the organization ahead of your personal agenda.

> ## When people respect you as a person, they admire you. When they respect you as a friend, they love you. When they respect you as a leader, they follow you.
>
> —JOHN C. MAXWELL

Pause for Reflection:

1. *Do you listen to and consider the input of your team members? How have you exhibited this practice for a recent decision?*

2. *Do your people trust and respect you?*

How to Hire the Right People

Jim Collins said, *"First* who, *then* what." He went on to say, "People are *not* your most important asset. The *right* people are." The key point he was making was that the "who" question came before the "what" decisions—before vision, before strategy, before organization structure, before tactics.

So how do we make sure we hire the right people? We can do this through intentional recruiting and by hiring people who work well together and share the same core values.

Recruiting, Selection, and Hiring

Prior to introducing our company's core values, we hired people more for their *competence* at the job being offered than for their *character* (their core values).

After introducing our core values, we became more intentional about hiring people first for their *character* (their core values) and then for their job *competence* and for their *chemistry,* asking ourselves, "Would they get along with our people?" We called this the 3 Cs, and I occasionally thought about a fourth C. I wish we had been more intentional about adding *capacity* (the person's ability to develop beyond the job being offered) to our list of primary hiring considerations.

We learned to wait to hire the right person even when we needed someone quickly. After we hired the *right* person, we worked hard to get them into the right *position* so they would be successful.

Our new employee orientation reinforced our core values and helped solidify the employees' understanding of the company. One of the cornerstones of our onboarding process was our "Albert Trolley History Tour." The tour was part of a multiday introduction and orientation and one of my favorite times to be involved. We would ride a rented trolley-like bus around the city, and I shared lots of stories covering the history of our company as we visited our various physical locations going back to 1938. I shared traditions that have made our company special and in doing so gave our new people the company's roots as a foundation. This tour created a special opportunity for me to connect with our new employees. They heard and saw my excitement and pride about where we had been and where we were going. Plus, they heard me talk about and saw me exhibit our core values, purpose, vision, and objectives.

It was also a time for our new hires to begin to understand whether they really fit into our company or not. And if not, this was the right time to leave our company so they could go and be successful with another.

The ERC confirms these practices:

Great workplaces hire the best—and only the best. They recognize that a great workplace and culture results from great people. They define the talent they need, strategically recruit it, and put into place selection practices that identify top performers, as well as onboarding practices that engage top performers and set them up for success from the start.

Within great workplaces, top performers work alongside other top performers who are positive, hardworking, committed and loyal, believe in what the organization does, and participate in making the workplace great.[10]

This simple change—being more intentional about hiring people first for their character—transformed our company. How? Because we attracted and hired a group of people who shared our core values. This common foundation enabled our people to become top performers who knew how to behave as they pursued our purpose, vision, objectives, and strategies.

We did not need bureaucratic rules and policies to tell our people how to behave. Why? Because we hired the *right* people who already possessed our core values. Their core values served as a guide for their decisions and behavior.

Likewise, the people you select as team members have a significant impact on your organizational culture. Even if it takes a little longer to find the right people instead of the "right now" people, I encourage you to stay true to your core values and choose only the best fit for your organization.

Pause for Reflection:

1. *Do you have a hiring process that allows you to hire the best people?*

2. *Once you select and hire the best, how does your orientation process prepare them to succeed in your organization?*

3. *Have you successfully formed a team of high performers in your workplace?*

---

[10] Ibid.

Investments with Big Returns
Training and Development

Ever since I was very young, I've been intensely curious. When I was a small boy, I would ride my little bicycle slowly around my neighborhood, just looking around. I ventured much farther from home than my parents ever knew, driven by my thirst to learn and discover new things. My curiosity has fueled my passion for personal growth, and so I've lived a life full of learning.

In addition, for as long as I can remember, I've wanted to add value to others. But I've discovered that you must grow yourself before you can grow others! So my pursuit of personal growth actually prepared me to develop the people around me.

One of the best ways to add value to others is through training and development. This direct investment in others will yield dividends (for you and them) for years to come!

As the ERC reports:

Great workplaces invest in training and development for their workforce to grow their talents and capabilities. They make time for learning and support it by paying for employees to participate in various opportunities and offering/delivering a variety of training and career development programs.[11]

In our company, we developed a leadership principle that we called **"ON/IN."** It meant to work *on* the business while you worked *in* the business.

Since we were in the moving and storage business, our peak season was the summer months between school years. It was a time of heavy working *in* the business. During this time, we would ask our people to take

---

[11] Ibid.

note of things that we could improve upon and could work *on* during our nonpeak season.

Many companies lay off people during their nonpeak seasons, but I chose to invest in our people. During the nonpeak season, ON/IN meant that I grew as a leader while we grew our people and our business. We filled our time with lots of training and development—building for our next peak season.

One secret I learned early in our business was that when we grew our people, they would help us grow our business. That is how we grew from five employees to over 150 by the time I sold the company.

We had not only skills training for our people but also training to help them become better people, better moms and dads, better friends, and better servants in our community. We had book reviews to encourage personal learning and group development. And we reinforced and lived out this principle through education assistance. We reimbursed up to $500 of tuition costs for those who continued their education at a university or college and had a grade average of C or higher.

Wise leaders look at training, development, and education as investments, not expenses.

Open Communication

Years ago, I discovered that good communication is necessary for effective leadership. A leader always sets the expectations and defines the level of communication by example, which means that if there are communication breakdowns in your organization, first examine the ways that you communicate. You communicate daily in any number of ways, and each instance is an opportunity to convey the other principles we have been discussing—such as your genuine concern and respect.

The motivation to communicate well is clear. In fact, studies have shown a direct relationship between open communication and increased performance in organizations. More specifically, every leader can develop a great workplace by incorporating effective communication into his or her culture.

The ERC noted the following about great workplaces:

Leaders frequently share information about the organization's performance, its financials, the vision and direction of the organization, and other critical information and updates at great workplaces. In addition, leaders regularly interact with and communicate with employees one-on-one, in small groups, and as an entire staff. Additionally, great workplaces help everyone understand the mission and purpose of the organization, and how their work connects to the big picture.[12]

Early on, I realized that a breakdown in communication often led to a breakdown in our business, but open and intentional communication enhanced mutual understanding within our organization. Over the next few decades, we used a variety of methods and events to sustain an environment of open communication:

- From 1989, we started every company-wide meeting by reminding our people of our mission and beliefs.

- Beginning in 1992, we shut down the company for half of a day once or twice in the fall just to learn and discuss the particular focus for the next year.

- We had three "State of the Company" meetings: one going into our peak season, one coming out, and one after the first of the year. We would talk about where we had been, where we were now, and where we were going. This was a great time to build trust and ownership with our people as we shared the details about our current situation and future direction.

---

[12] Ibid.

- Going into our peak season, we did the "Trolley History Tour" I described before. The tour helped our new team members quickly connect with the purpose and vision of our organization.

- Prior to having our Friday Stand-Up meetings, I would use payroll envelope stuffers to consistently communicate about what was going on in the company and to remind our people about the focus for the year.

- Each month at our Friday Stand-Up meetings, we would communicate our financial progress toward the threshold for our Pay for Performance incentive/bonus.

- Finally, there was no substitute for Management By Walking Around. It was amazing what I learned as I just asked questions and listened to our people. And best of all, our employees knew I was interested in what they were doing and cared about each of them as a person.

Pause for Reflection:

1. *How does your company encourage personal growth, learning, and training?*

2. *How do you communicate with your team?*

3. *What challenges do you face when it comes to regular, open communication?*

As leaders, we have a great opportunity to shape our culture by the way we communicate with our team. Even a small positive change to your normal communication routine can be very noticeable and can open the door to bigger and better results.

In the next chapter, we will dive deeper into the importance of intentionally evaluating and strengthening your workplace culture—and how to maximize your impact and empower your team in the process.

CHAPTER NINE:
Serve Your People, Strengthen Your Culture

EMPLOY YOUR LEADERSHIP TO SERVE OTHERS AND ENHANCE YOUR WORKPLACE CULTURE

"To win in the marketplace you must first win in the workplace."

DOUG CONANT

L et's take a closer look at actions you can take to improve your workplace culture, building it into something great and inspiring. This has positive repercussions at every level of your organization.

As another step in this direction, I'd like to share with you a leadership secret—a way to boost the morale of your team and motivate them toward excellence. This one behavior can supercharge your team like perhaps no other aspect of leadership!

The Power of Praise

Spend an afternoon at any elementary-age athletic event, and I guarantee the loudest sounds you hear will come from the parents in the bleachers next to you. As little Susie drives for the goal or little Johnny heads into his last lap, excited parents will cheer like a new world record is about to be made:

"You can do it! Keep going!"

And when the buzzer sounds or the trophies are handed out, smiling parents once again offer validation: "Great job. I knew you could do it."

Yes, the kids light up when they hear it. But as we reach adulthood, surely we have outgrown the need for such reassurance.

Haven't we?

According to a 2004 article, a Gallup survey of four million employees worldwide in over thirty different industries found that individuals who received regular recognition and praise showed higher individual productivity, higher engagement with colleagues, greater likelihood of staying with their organization, higher loyalty and satisfaction scores from customers, and better safety records.

The Employers Resource Council (ERC) reported a similar finding about great workplaces:

> Great workplaces show they appreciate and value employees and their contributions. They celebrate success often, and praise, recognize, and reward employees in a variety of formal and informal ways. They never miss an opportunity to say 'thanks' for employees' hard work.[13]

When I was a young leader, I developed the habit of looking for opportunities to publicly give someone credit for doing a great job. I always looked for a reason to recognize, praise, and say thank you to an employee.

---

[13] Ibid.

There are two ways to foster a habit of recognition: informal and formal. Both work very well when used regularly.

Informal Recognition

As a leader, I developed a casual but intentional habit of walking around and talking with our people. During these impromptu conversations, I would listen for positive accomplishments or look for notable behavior.

I'd then routinely compliment the positive behavior to the person and mention it to others in the company. This served to inspire the original person as well as the others to whom I described the behavior. My actions encouraged other employees to embrace that particular positive behavior since they knew it was valued.

If I heard Bruce say something positive about Jason, I would go to Jason and let him know about the positive thing that Bruce said about him. I became the conduit for positive affirmations and compliments, always ready to pass along and echo favorable comments. This really helped to align the team and increase employee satisfaction and morale.

Formal Recognition

Another way to encourage the habit of recognition is through formal awards. Our company set up a number of acknowledgments and awards to encourage and recognize our people. These practices and structures served to reinforce excellence and promote self-esteem throughout the entire organization.

Think about the structures in place in your organization to offer praise and recognition, and consider how you can expand them. To get you started, here's a list of ways in which our business recognized employees at company-wide meetings and gatherings. As you read it, think about how you could adapt and implement these techniques to serve the specifics of your own business.

- VIP (Values in Practice) Awards: Given from one employee to another when the first sees a company core value being displayed.

- Skill and the Will Awards: Given to an employee when a good remark comes from a customer.

- Length of Service Recognition: Given to employees in five-year increments.

- Department Goals Met: Recognized employees in the sales department and the operations department for meeting their respective departmental goals.

- Logbook Masters Awards: Recognized drivers when they submitted on-time, complete, and accurate logbooks.

- One-Degree Difference Maker Awards: Awarded by the Military/Government Traffic Department, cross-company, to determine who has made the biggest difference in that quarter.

- QIC Spotlight: Given when one employee wants to publicly say, "Thank you," to another employee.

Once you get your award systems defined and in place, they become guides that help you keep your team motivated and the company going in the right direction. As leaders, we have a great opportunity to shape our culture by the way we recognize and praise our team.

Pause for Reflection:

1. *How do you recognize, praise, and reward your team?*

2. *What award systems do you have in place to motivate and guide your team?*

What Does Dr. Seuss Know about Building an Inspiring Culture?

When leaders think about building great organizations with inspiring cultures, they usually don't consult children's books for guidance. But children's author Dr. Seuss revealed a key culture-building principle when he said, "Fun is good." The good doctor realized that fun is indeed a good thing. We have been talking about what a strong, inspiring culture looks like, and the ERC's report is once again helpful:

> Great workplaces have a unique culture that is their own, often described as fun, congenial, collaborative, positive, passionate, and creative. Their work environments, people, and workplace practices all help create a vibrant, positive, magnetic, and infectious culture.[14]

That description just sounds fun, doesn't it?

As of 2016, Google has been on *Fortune* magazine's list of "Top Companies to Work For" for the past ten years, occupying the number-one spot for seven of those years. Reportedly, employee perks include unlimited snacks and three organic meals per day, on-site oil changes, a spa truck, nap pods (for power naps), treadmill desks, garden space for growing vegetables, free fitness classes, and office and meeting rooms designed to resemble everything from a sidewalk café to ski gondolas. Undeniably, they have created a fun culture, backing up their claim that they want their workers to be employees for life—and to enjoy that life while they're at it.

You've likely heard the saying, "Families who play together stay together." Well, I would like to say that people in the workplace who play together stay together, and they develop a unified team spirit that cannot be broken.

---

[14] Ibid.

Over the years, we looked for any excuse to have some fun, especially during our summer peak season because of the pressure and stress our people bore during that time.

The objective of each fun activity was simple: to communicate to our people that we cared for them.

Here are a few ways our company had fun while showing appreciation (use it to spark your own ideas):

- Casual Fridays: Throughout the year, folks wore jeans with a company shirt on Friday.

- Chili Cook-Off: Employees competed for the best home-made chili. There were many different categories—best decoration, best chili, hottest chili, best name . . .

- Spring Softball: Employees and spouses played on an Albert-sponsored team.

- Spring Golf Scramble: Employees, customers, and suppliers played for prizes.

- Summer Peak-Season Happy Fridays: Food and events included Bahama Buck's snow cones, egg-on-a-spoon races, root beer floats, chocolate fountains, dessert contests, build-your-own ice cream sundaes, water-balloon tosses, chair massages, water-gun fights, burger cookouts, and an end-of-summer junk-car smashing.

- Bowling and Burgers: Teams competed for best team names and other fun prizes, such as Biggest Shoe, Loudest Dropped Ball, Best Gutter Ball, etc.

- Thanksgiving Potluck Lunch: Employees signed up to bring their favorite dish.

- Kids' Day: Children and grandchildren of employees were invited to our business to see where Mom or Dad or a grand-parent worked. We had food and games, and the Christmas story was told.

- Poinsettias: Placed on each desk and throughout the company.
- Christmas Lunch: Celebrated the season.
- Random Holiday Celebrations: National Donut Day, Chocolate Day, Chocolate Chip Cookie Day, and more!

When I was not traveling for business, I participated like a kid in a candy store (my favorite activity was the water-gun fights). As leaders, we have a great opportunity to shape our culture by the way we have fun with our team. You'll lead more effectively when you realize that having fun in the workplace refreshes your people and draws them together as a team.

I believe every leader can improve his or her culture by incorporating fun into the workplace. I've also learned that we have to be intentional about our fun making. Dr. Seuss puts it this way: "It's fun to have fun, but you have to know how."

Pause for Reflection:

1. *How do you have fun with your team?*

2. *Could you boost the morale and outlook of your team by getting intentional about planning a fun event for your team members?*

An Uncommon Way to Grow Your Business

Have you ever been asked to serve your community or a nonprofit organization in a volunteer capacity? I've had this happen several times, and my answers to this question have significantly impacted me as well as my company.

When we are asked to help out, we often hesitate and wonder whether we have the time to devote to something that is not a regular part of life or business. After all, time spent serving in a nonprofit organization is time that could be otherwise spent growing our own businesses. But our business never seemed to be hurt because of the time I spent serving other people outside our business. In fact, I have discovered some distinct benefits to serving in nonprofit organizations.

Great Workplaces

Over the years, I have really enjoyed community service and have been involved in so many ways. In fact, the leadership practice of serving in your community corresponds with another attribute in the ERC report on great workplaces:

> Great workplaces make an impact on and give back to their local community. Not only do they generously donate their company resources to the community, but they also serve their communities by helping others in need and offering their staff's time and talents.[15]

This means that every leader can improve his or her culture by incorporating community service into the workplace.

Because I had such good experience in serving our community, I was always encouraging our people to serve as well. I not only tried to set an example but also offered our business services free or at cost when we identified a worthy need. For example, in the twelve-month period before I sold our company, we engaged our employees and our company to donate time and/or money to twelve different organizations, and we donated in-kind goods and services to thirty-nine different organizations.

This focus on serving others benefited the community and our employees. Our service in and to our community had the following impacts:

---

[15] Ibid.

- Our employees learned how to work with a wide variety of people to accomplish a common objective.

- The community thought well of our employees and our business. Our reputation was held in high esteem. Because of our good reputation:

  o Our business continued to grow.

  o It was easier to recruit good employees.

- Our employees developed tighter bonds with each other and became a more cohesive team.

- Our employees thought well of our company because we used our business to better the community their families lived in. Therefore, it made it easier to retain good employees.

Even a small act of kindness and service can cause a big chain reaction. Volunteering in your community is not only a great way to give back but also a great way to build relationships with your employees and with the people you serve.

Pause for Reflection:

1. *How do you, your employees, and your business serve your community?*

2. *Can you think of one way to incorporate the practice of serving others into your workplace culture?*

Six Ways to Achieve Work–Life Balance

Have you ever had an employee who failed to perform at his highest level because of personal problems? It can be frustrating when someone's personal life impacts his professional life in a negative way. Many employers simply tell their people to keep their personal problems out of the workplace. But there's a problem with that approach.

Ultimately, you cannot separate a person's work life from his personal life. Trying to do so will frustrate you and alienate your employee. Instead of seeking to separate an employee's personal life from his work life, I've learned that it's best to acknowledge that work and life are intertwined. Once we understand that work and life are inseparable, we can then lead our people in ways that support them at work and at home.

Work-Life Balance

Tightrope walking—also called funambulism, from the Greek words for "rope" and "to walk"—dates back to ancient Greece and Rome, where these stunning acrobats were revered. The practice has endured for millennia and remains popular: in 1974, Philippe Petit famously walked a wire stretched between the World Trade Center's Twin Towers, and in 2013, Nik Wallenda crossed a cable spanning a 1,400-foot-wide gorge near the Grand Canyon at a height of 1,500 feet (taller than the Empire State Building), also without harness or net. Across the centuries, the key to a successful high-wire act has been the same:

Balance.

Without it, none of us could function successfully, whether crossing a rope or juggling multiple competing responsibilities. The ERC report is again helpful here:

> Great workplaces are flexible to employees' work/life needs and encourage work/life balance by offering flexible schedules, providing generous paid time off, accommodating individual requests and needs, and creating a supportive work environment that is understanding of personal and family obligations.[16]

---

[16] Ibid.

As a key leader in your company, you may be wondering what you can do to support and encourage a healthy work–life balance in your workplace. It turns out there are multiple ways to show and communicate your support to your people. Here are some ways that we have encouraged work–life balance in our company:

- We did not penalize or discipline employees for occasional attendance issues, especially when the employee's work was completed on time and with excellence.

- We monitored and reviewed employees' workloads to help ensure that they were not overloaded and could maintain work–life balance.

- We asked employees to work with their managers concerning their schedule to solve their work–life issues.

- We modified work schedules to give people part-time options, plus the ability to arrive early or late. We permitted them to attend appointments or miss work without using paid time off (PTO) or vacation time.

- We had a generous PTO / vacation / sick-time policy and also allowed them to bank unused time. We also provided paid holidays, bereavement leave, jury duty leave, and leave of absence.

- Since our business had a peak season during the summer months, we had a PTO calendar to help people schedule their family vacations. This helped them understand when we had the greatest need for all hands on deck and when they could relax with their families.

As leaders, we can improve our culture by encouraging work–life balance in the workplace. You'll lead more effectively when your team knows you care about all aspects of their lives.

Pause for Reflection:

1. *How do you encourage work—life balance for your team?*

The Benefits of Healthy Employees

In 1982, I weighed 238 pounds and was out of shape. Through diet and exercise, I lost thirty pounds in thirty days, fifty pounds in six months, and seventy pounds in one year! I also completed two Olympic-distance triathlons during that time.

I kept bicycling and have logged about one hundred thousand miles to date. When I don't cycle, I go on four- to seven-mile walks to keep up my routine of exercising six days a week. Wellness remains one of my top priorities. And I encourage my employees to lead healthy, active lifestyles, too.

> It is health that is real wealth and
> not pieces of gold and silver.
>
> —MAHATMA GANDHI

Numerous Benefits

Wellness in the workplace is important for you, your employees, *and* your organization. The same principles that transformed me can transform your organization. If you can help your employees improve their overall well-being in a holistic way (mind, body, spirit, and emotion), they will:

- Develop higher self-esteem.

- Be more confident in who they are.

- Be more content with what they have.

- Become courageous in how they live their life.

Now, do I need to tell you how productive and customer-centric employees would be if they had *confidence, contentment,* and *courage?*

Emphasizing wellness in the workplace corresponds with another attribute in the ERC report:

> Great workplaces genuinely care about their employees' well-being. They offer wellness options that help employees develop healthy lifestyle behaviors as well as provide an array of benefits, which support their employees' health and personal welfare.[17]

The following are a few ways our company helped employees to develop healthy lifestyles and behaviors:

- Wellness Fair: Once a year, we brought in health-care providers as part of our wellness fair. They taught our people about healthy living and provided a variety of free health screenings.

- Move It and Lose It: Once or twice a year, we had weight-loss contests.

- Flu Shots: Each fall, we had a health-care provider come on-site to provide the shots. We encouraged our people to save their off days for vacation and not for sickness. The shots were for the whole family so our employees could avoid being off due to sick family members.

- Fitness Gym Memberships: We paid 50 percent of memberships.

- "Drink before you're thirsty, and eat before you're hungry": Beginning each May, we conducted a training session with our local moving crews on hydration and how foods impact the body. Throughout our peak summer season and during our

---

[17] Ibid.

Texas triple-digit temperatures, we provided our crews with large jugs of ice and water or a sports drink and fruit to eat.

- Emotional Health: We were proactive in helping our people deal with their emotional health. We paid particular attention to our team members during our busy, more stressful peak seasons.

- Chaplains: We subscribed to an employee-assistance program called Marketplace Chaplains. These chaplains made weekly worksite visits and were available to our employees and their families 24–7.

As leaders, we have a great opportunity to improve our culture by encouraging wellness with our team. You'll lead more effectively when your people see that you care about them and their wellness.

When you have your health, you have everything. When you do not have your health, nothing else matters at all.

—AUGUSTEN BURROUGHS

Pause for Reflection:

1. *How do you promote wellness with your team?*

2. *How can you do even more to lead a healthier lifestyle?*

Addressing the Emotional and Spiritual Needs of Your Team

The backbone of your workplace culture is the people who work with and for you. And your people have many needs. Some can be characterized as physical needs, while others are emotional or spiritual in nature. At times, people encounter some tough "valleys" as they walk through this life.

I cared about my people so much, and they knew they could come to me when they were struggling and needed help or guidance. It wasn't long before I realized I was getting over my head. As the boss, I understood that they shouldn't be sharing these personal matters with me. I didn't want it to tarnish my perception of their potential and performance as an employee. And apart from that, some of these were major issues that would have been better shared with a counselor.

I understood that in order to build the type of culture I desired, I needed help. That's when we partnered with Marketplace Chaplains to help meet the emotional and spiritual needs of our people.

Many people associate a chaplain with a military pastor, but this chaplain service is for the workplace. So what are Marketplace Chaplains, and what do they do?

- A 24–7 employee-assistance program called Chaplain Care Program.

- Founded on the US military chaplain model.

- Built on regularly scheduled, weekly worksite visits without interrupting work, and *confidential* and trusting relationships with employees and their families.

- Serving in over one thousand US cities and in five foreign countries.

- Providing guidance or help when events, such as crises or tragedies, occur in our lives and we need someone to turn to.

- Encouraging and calming people, chaplains offer emotional support or provide referrals to social service agencies or employee-assistance programs.

As the owner, I was happy to listen to my employees, but I was not at all qualified to counsel them through major life crises. As much as I wanted to help each person, I simply didn't have the knowledge, the expertise, or the bandwidth to take on the role of a personal counselor. Marketplace Chaplains was the ideal solution to my problem.

I think every leader should subscribe to the Chaplain Care Program for the following three reasons.

1. Employees Win

The first reason to use this program is that it helps your employees. Here are some of the ways I saw our chaplains help our employees:

- Our chaplain jumped in with full effort to care for the employees and families impacted by a tragic local truck accident in which two of our employees died and a third was severely injured.

- An employee's boyfriend was about to commit suicide when she got our chaplain involved in the middle of the night and saved his life.

- One employee said the chaplain saved his marriage.

- Employees (and even former employees) have had our chaplain conduct weddings for them and funerals for family members.

- One of our chaplains helped an employee cope with the aftermath of rape.

Our chaplains were there to comfort our people in times of crisis, hold their hands in times of mourning, and also lead them in times of celebration. Each time, the chaplains were able to help out in ways above and beyond what I could have done. I am forever grateful for their professionalism and passion in helping people.

2. Customers and Suppliers Win

The second reason to use Marketplace Chaplains is to help meet the needs of your customers and suppliers. Often, our customers were under a lot of stress. Many were taking new jobs and had to uproot their families in order to move to the new place of employment. Some were moving because of divorce or death in the family.

We moved people all over the nation, from coast to coast. Our company frequently used other moving and storage companies (suppliers) to help service our customers in various markets across the country. These suppliers were a key part of how we served our customers, so we decided to extend the chaplain service to these two key groups.

They offered their help:

- To a customer who was stressed over a move by offering to come by the customer's home to talk about life issues.

- To suppliers who had crises concerning an employee. For example, one time a supplier had an over-the-road driver who ran over and killed a person who stepped out in front of his truck on the interstate. We were able to send a chaplain to be on-site with the driver because he was understandably devastated.

3. The Company Wins

The third reason to use the Chaplain Care Program is that Marketplace Chaplains will help *your company*. We started using this program to meet needs that we saw in our employees', customers', and suppliers' lives. We had no idea how the program would positively affect our company, but it did!

The Chaplain Care Program helped us achieve:

- Increased employee retention.

- Decreased employee absenteeism.

- Increased employee productivity.

- Improved workplace safety.

- Reduced employee stress.

- Increased employee commitment to company goals and objectives.

- Reduced employee conflicts.

- Increased employee loyalty to the company.

- Improved employee attitudes.

- Increased employee morale and teamwork.

- Increased employee feelings of being valued.

If you stop and think about it, I bet you'll conclude that this service is one of the best ways to help employees, customers, and suppliers when they are in need. And in helping all of those people get what they need, you help yourself by being able to shift the heavy load of *counselor* to individuals who are far more equipped than you.

Pause for Reflection:

1. *How do you help your team deal with the emotional and spiritual needs and crises that occur in their lives?*

2. *Can you think of a way that a chaplain program could be used at your place of business?*

Achieve Gold-Medal Results

There's nothing quite like the smile on an athlete who has just competed with the best of the best and won an Olympic gold medal. They *know* that they competed with excellence. While most of us have not won an Olympic medal, we all know the sense of satisfaction that comes from doing an excellent job.

The Olympics started in Greece, and I like what Aristotle, the famous Greek philosopher and scientist, had to say about excellence: "We are what we repeatedly do. Excellence, then, is not an act but a habit." Aristotle knew that what we do habitually—what becomes ingrained in the core of who we are and is a part of our daily living-out of our values—is what defines our pursuit of excellence, not the chance victory or defeat.

Great workplaces create an atmosphere where this habitual pursuit of excellence is nurtured and top performance is recognized as ongoing dedication rather than a one-time event. As the ERC notes:

> Through performance management practices that help guide, support, and develop exceptional performance, great workplaces provide clarity on how to be a top performer, help other employees become top performers, and assist existing top performers in sustaining top performance. Reaching for excellence each and every day is what makes great workplaces successful.[18]

Excellence isn't a sometime thing; it's an all-time thing.

I can attest to those results in my own organization. It's clear that excellence in the workplace is a great attribute that we should all aspire to. The question for leaders becomes, "How can I encourage and instill excellence in my organization?" Here are three ways you can encourage excellence in your company:

---

[18] Ibid.

1. **Through clearly expressed values.** If one of your core values is excellence, peak performance, or a similar value, emphasize this value at every opportunity. One of our core values was "Strive for Excellence," and this value was posted prominently, taught at company-wide events, and routinely referenced as a defining core value for the company.

2. **By example.** Most principles are better caught than taught. When people see their leader working with excellence, it's easier to perform their own duties with excellence. I believe each of us should set the bar higher for ourselves than anybody else will.

3. **By internal initiatives.** As mentioned, we developed an internal initiative that we called ON/IN. It simply stated, "Work *on* the business while we work *in* the business." Working *on* the business meant growing myself, growing our people, and growing our business.

Warning: since I was very young, I have tried to do things with excellence. But one thing I have learned about myself is that when I "strive for excellence" too strongly, I can cross the line into perfectionism. And when I cross that line, there are "dead bodies" (employees and family members) lying around me, and everyone winds up frustrated. So be aware of where that line is in your own life.

Leaders, you can set the standard for excellence by how you go about your work. I've learned that we have to be intentional about having an attitude of excellence. With some thoughtful planning, you can communicate your expectations of excellence and develop some codified approaches that will move everyone toward the gold-medal podium.

If you don't have time to do it right, when will you have the time to do it over?

—JOHN WOODEN

Pause for Reflection:

1. *How does your behavior encourage excellence in your organization?*

2. *What systems or processes do you have in place to stimulate and reward excellence?*

The Key to Keeping Your Customers

Think about the last time you ate at a restaurant where the service was poor. If you take a moment, a memory probably comes to mind—maybe you waited forever to have your drink order taken, or the wrong food was delivered, or you were treated rudely. If you're like me, the poor service affected your overall impression of the business, even how the food tasted! Now, you'll probably also agree that *great service* makes the whole meal more enjoyable.

CX Act, formerly TARP Worldwide (Technical Assistance Research Programs), conducted a survey to understand why customers leave businesses, and the results are interesting.

Reason for Leaving	Percentage
Poor service	68%
Unhappy with product	14%
Lured away by competition	9%
Influenced by a friend	5%
Moved away	3%
Died	1%

As you can see, when it comes to keeping customers, *how we serve them* is over four times more important than *what we actually sell* as a product or service! It's pretty clear that in order for our organizations to thrive, we have to focus on customer service.

A leadership focus on exceptional customer service and quality in the workplace also contributes to a winning culture. The ERC report outlines this fact:

> Great workplaces are successful, growing, and innovative. They hold themselves to high standards, are focused on delivering exceptional customer service and quality, and strive to innovate and continuously improve their organizations. They are always raising the bar in their businesses and in their workplaces.[19]

If we are going to serve our customers well, it has to start with our key leaders. But leaders are busy with their important day-to-day duties. So how do leaders find time to create a culture that supports and encourages excellent customer service? By addressing the following three areas in their organization:

1. Awareness

To reach a solution for any problem, the first step is always to reach an awareness that the problem exists. The same goes for grasping hold of opportunities. In the same way, leaders need to be aware of the importance of customer service before their workplace culture can truly prioritize it. If you don't understand that this is a crucial part of your business, nothing will change.

You also need to be aware of the place you are starting from. Study those parts of your organization that deal with customer service. Analyze what you are doing well and learn which aspects can be improved. Talk

---

[19] Ibid.

to those on the front lines and benefit from their experience and insights. Keep digging until you have a full picture of how customer service is currently valued, taught, rewarded, and implemented at your organization.

2. High-Level Messaging

One area for leaders to target with their customer-service emphasis is the high-level messaging of the organization. Here is an example from our company: our purpose statement, "Customers for Life," reflects our desire to develop and sustain long-term customer relationships. This defines *why we exist* as a company.

I also took this further to include our suppliers. I wanted us to help our suppliers to be the best they could be so they could help us serve our customers with exceptional service and quality.

3. Ways and Approaches

Every organization has its *way* of doing things. It also has certain methods of approaching business challenges, suppliers, employees, and customers. Oftentimes, these ways and approaches are not written down; they just exist by means of repeated behaviors.

In our company, we realized that our impact on the market would be the result of what thinking, processes, and behaviors we repeated on a daily basis. Instead of just letting these important behaviors randomly happen, we decided to codify our desired ways of thinking and doing into our ways and approaches. Here is one that relates to customer service:

EEE (Triple E): Give customers an Experience that Exceeds their Expectations. When we meet customers' expectations, we have just satisfied them. However, when we exceed the customers' expectations, we have *delighted* them.

I suspect you'll have your own unique high-level messages and ways and approaches to serving your customers, but the important thing is to be intentional about this area of your business. When you draw your blueprint for customer service and use it to lead your people, you'll have a clear plan to follow as you take your business to the next level.

Pause for Reflection:

1. *How do you encourage an attitude of exceptional customer service within your team?*

2. *Do you have a defined strategy for modeling, teaching, and reinforcing extraordinary quality and customer service in your organization?*

As we wrap up this important section on culture, I want to ensure, once again, that it is set in the proper context for your ultimate success. It bears repeating that culture is the fruit, not the goal, so the inspiring culture that you seek will not fully develop by merely striving to have a better culture! If you really want to hit the ball out of the park with your workplace culture, you need to operate and lead from a firm foundation.

That foundation has three main parts: clearly identified values, a compelling purpose, and a clear vision of where you want to go. When you get these right and lead with a values-driven approach, you'll be well on your way to fostering the inspiring culture that you desire.

Like a train that crawls out of the station to eventually build up a sustainable momentum, it takes less energy and effort to keep the train moving once it is at cruising speed. In the next chapter, we're going to look at ways to keep your values-driven culture on track and moving forward!

PART VI
GOALS AND CONTROLS

CHAPTER TEN:
Tap the Power of Goals

"All good performance starts with clear goals."

KEN BLANCHARD

O n May 25, 1961, President John F. Kennedy held the attention of the nation as he spoke before a joint session of Congress and declared the following:

"I believe that this nation should commit itself to achieving the goal, before this decade is out, of landing a man on the moon and returning him safely to the earth. No single space project in this period will be more impressive to mankind, or more important for the long-range exploration of space; and none will be so difficult or expensive to accomplish."

President Kennedy did not sugarcoat the "very heavy costs" this would incur, and he stressed: "If we are to go only half way, or reduce our sights in the face of difficulty, in my judgment it would be better not to go at all." There would be no sense in pursuing this goal, he said, "unless we are prepared to do the work and bear the burdens to make it successful."

Billions of dollars and eight years later, after countless hours spent developing the equipment and processes that would carry the Apollo 11 team to the moon and back, the world breathlessly watched as history was made. One giant leap for mankind, indeed.

Goals and Controls

How about you—would you like to see your organization take a giant leap in performance and results? I propose that your organization needs someone to count the cost, set an inspiring goal, and cast the vision, just like Kennedy did for our nation.

Business does not always resemble space exploration; in many ways, business is more like warfare. In both cases, someone needs to step up and propose a strategy that brings success and victory. And it needs to be the *right* strategy. That someone is you, the leader.

I've observed that successful organizations share the following characteristics:

- Clear, stretching goals.

- Can-do atmosphere.

- People displaying a high sense of urgency.

- Skills to implement plan-oriented actions.

- Ability to achieve dependable results.

It all comes down to goals *and* controls. So what are goals and controls?

Goals

Achievement and recognition of achievement are two of the best motivators around. The goals of individuals and the group must be clearly defined, understood, and—to be fully beneficial—accepted as reasonable. They must be:

- Specific.
- Vital.
- Measurable.
- Achievable.
- Challenging.
- Time-bound.

Controls

Organizations are formed to get results. People are hired to get results. And supervisors and managers are recruited to get results and to assist others in getting results. Once the processes for establishing goals are set, the processes of following up and following through on the tactical projects and goals are then needed.

This requires:

- Frequent and regular communication reporting on the progress of those tactical projects and goals.
- Intentional communication to ensure your people's progress on objectives and strategies is in alignment with your values, purpose, and vision.

Insight: The *way* leaders approach goals and controls is as important as the goals and controls themselves.

Clearly, goals are necessary if we are to reach our full potential. How we think about, set, and *monitor our progress* toward our goals—through controls— is vitally important.

Do you want your organization to achieve more? If so, then the ideas discussed here can serve as your launchpad to greater success!

Pause for Reflection:

1. *How do you set and use goals in your business?*

2. *How do you monitor your progress as you work toward your goals?*

A Leadership Lesson from Albert Einstein

A few years ago, a friend shared a story he heard Billy Graham tell as the keynote speaker honoring the delegates to the United Nations in New York:

Being here in New York reminds me of a story about Albert Einstein. Some years ago, the great thinker was on a train bound for New York City.

As the ticket taker came walking through the car, Einstein reached into his pocket to retrieve his ticket, but he could not find it. He frantically searched his coat pockets, turned his pants pockets inside out, but still he could not produce the ticket.

The ticket taker said, "Don't worry, Mr. Einstein, we all know who you are. Forget about it." About twenty minutes later, the ticket taker came back through the car, and by this time, Einstein was on the floor searching everywhere for the lost ticket.

Again the ticket taker tried to reassure Einstein by saying, "I told you not to worry about the lost ticket. We trust that you purchased one, and that's good enough for us."

Einstein looked up at the railroad employee and said, "Young man, this isn't a matter of trust but of direction. I need to find the ticket because I forgot where I'm going."

Do you know where you're going? Are you headed toward your destination? Successful people know where they are going. And they have a plan for getting there.

> # Give me a stock clerk with a goal, and I will give you a man who will make history. Give me a man without a goal, and I will give you a stock clerk.
>
> —J.C. PENNEY

My good friend and mentor Jim Lundy would often say:

> If you don't know where you are going,
>
> Any path will get you there,
>
> But you won't realize if you're lost,
>
> You won't know what time you'll arrive,
>
> You won't know the dimensions of your challenge,
>
> Others won't understand how they could help,
>
> And since you could pass right by without recognizing it,
>
> You won't get the satisfaction of having arrived!

I learned in my early working years that it was important for me, as the leader, to *pause, reflect,* and *plan* so I knew where I was going. But I also learned that it was even more important to get every employee involved in the *planning* and *decision-making* process so we would go down the right road together.

Such thinking, planning, and decision making serves to clarify the direction of the entire team. Likewise, you and your team can reach your destination with greater efficiency and momentum by avoiding ambiguous goals.

Ambiguous Goals

Imagine that you are at a family-reunion picnic and you decide to try your hand at a game of archery. You select your bow and receive as many arrows as you wish. Yet when you step up to the line, you notice there is no target in sight. Then someone who is overseeing the game says, "OK, select an arrow, draw your bow, and shoot!"

What do you do next? Do you just stand there waiting for further instructions? With no defined target, I bet you would hesitate to draw your bow.

But let's say you shoot one arrow just to see what happens. When you shoot, you learn what it feels like when the target is out of sight or undefined.

Without the feedback of seeing how close you came to the target, you could not adjust your aim in order to hit closer to the bull's-eye. Because there is no bull's-eye! You would have no way of knowing whether you even came close to hitting the target. In other words, you could not gauge your level of success.

Insight: Ambiguous goals in the workplace and inadequate feedback lead to confusion and frustration.

Achievement and recognition are two of the best motivators. And leaders should provide their people with a chance to seek and achieve fulfillment in their work. But first, the goals determining where you are going must be clearly defined, understood, and accepted as reasonable in order to be fully beneficial.

Employees need goals so they can correct their actions when targets are missed and so they can feel the deserved satisfaction when targets are hit. They also need a clear path that outlines where they are going.

Einstein is best known for his groundbreaking work in physics. But his reaction to a lost train ticket reflected an even more fundamental truth: knowing your destination is of the utmost importance. We can apply the same truth to our lives and leadership.

Pause for Reflection:

1. *Where does your ticket say you are going?*

2. *Do you have clearly defined goals in your life and in your workplace?*

Are You a Lone Ranger When Setting Goals?

For years, I was "Mr. Idea Man" in our company. But that was my job, wasn't it? As the leader of the company, I thought it was my duty to generate the ideas and map out how to implement them. Eventually, I learned that there was a *better* way to lead my team—a method for increasing innovation and managing change at the same time.

My old management style went something like this. When I got an idea for our business, I would come up with all of the questions to ask and do all of the research to determine all the answers. Then I would go to our management team to present my idea and explain how it would work. The team always accepted the ideas, but they were always "Bobby's ideas."

For days, weeks, and even months after I presented an idea, I found myself spending a lot of time and energy just persuading my team that it was a good idea. And when it came time to implement a "Bobby idea," the process was very slow, and it always took a lot of pushing and prodding to make it happen. It was draining and discouraging.

Observation: The more competent a manager is in the technical aspect of his or her work, the stronger the tendency is for the manager to make decisions and set goals alone and then simply tell employees what to do.

Are you a Lone Ranger when it comes to making decisions and even setting goals in your organization, like I was?

In most organizations, goals are often imposed from the top of the organization onto those below. With this top-down approach, leaders usually find their goal-oriented system isn't working right, and the following symptoms appear:

- People consider goal setting and planning as a periodic exercise rather than a way of life.

- They consider the whole approach somewhat of a nuisance because of the overemphasis on elaborate details and page after page of forms.

- The goals are regarded as arbitrarily imposed.

- The planning cycle is usually completed several weeks late. Then, employees wipe their brows and say, "Whew! Now that we've finished that exercise, let's get back to getting our work done."

But think about it—even the Lone Ranger wasn't really a loner. Everywhere he went, he rode with Tonto! I needed other people to help me get the job done. Andrew Carnegie said it well: "Teamwork is the ability to work together toward a common vision. . . . It is the fuel that allows common people to attain uncommon results."

You can improve your team's performance by asking three key questions when setting goals. At the very *beginning* of the goal-setting process—and *before* defining any team or company goals—the empowering leader seeks input from his or her employees. Such a leader asks:

1. *Who* can help me set a better goal?

2. *Who* will have to carry it out?

3. *Who* will be impacted by it?

When you, as the leader, use these three questions to gather input from your team members, they have a better understanding of and commitment to the goals *that you collaboratively set.* And they take pride in the achievement of goals when they are involved in the development, creation, and implementation *planning* stages.

When employees provide the necessary input, how can they complain about implementing their own plans?

And as the leader, you can avoid having those who:

- Lack a feeling of ownership or commitment.

- Drag their heels in implementation.

- Resort to sabotaging the plans.

Comment: This is NOT goal setting by a committee. The leader must still decide the future direction and goal(s) for the organization.

When you lay down your Lone Ranger mask and give your people a chance to participate in the decision-making and goal-setting processes, they have a real opportunity to gain experience and grow professionally.

Pause for Reflection:

1. *Are you a Lone Ranger when setting goals?*

2. *Would you like to have a more team-oriented approach to your goal-setting process?*

Is Your Goal Setting Top-Down or Bottom-Up? (The Answer May Surprise You)

As I mentioned earlier, I love bicycling. And I love watching the Tour de France, the Super Bowl of cycling. The Tour is an annual twenty-one-stage race over three weeks of furious cycling, primarily held in France. In 2015, it was mountain-heavy and covered over two thousand miles with only two rest days. One thing I know is that herculean challenges like the Tour provide some great lessons about teamwork and leadership.

With arms over each other's shoulders, linked together for their slow-motion victorious finish, second-time Tour winner Chris Froome and his cycling teammates pedaled over the finish line on the Champs-Élysées in Paris. Even though Froome won the Tour that year as an individual, it took a *team* to support him.

Speaking about his team (the other cyclists, the bicycling maintenance people, the team chef, the race team director, etc.), Froome said, "This is your yellow jersey as much as it is mine."

The television commentators on NBCSN would often say that any member on Froome's cycling team was so talented that they could lead their own cycling team.

Froome knew how to win championships. He also knew where his strength and support came from.

> ## Everybody on the championship team doesn't get publicity, but everyone can say he's a champion.
> —EARVIN "MAGIC" JOHNSON

How to Win Championships

Those who win championships understand that the first and most fundamental step toward success is to surround themselves with highly motivated people who form a high-performance *team* and who have a can-do spirit. In an organization, the equivalent is a culture in which superior performance has become a habit.

People like to feel good about themselves. And the most surefire way for people to feel good about themselves is to have a sense of achievement and recognition for the goals they have achieved.

Since success has been defined as the achievement of one or more predetermined goals, goal setting is the logical starting point for an achievement journey. So should planning and goal setting happen from the top down or the bottom up?

The answer is *yes!* The goal-setting process should be based on dialogues, not monologues.

Insight: Leaders in pursuit of peak-performance teams have learned that how goals are determined is as important as the clarity of the goals themselves.

People don't like performing for arbitrary authority figures. When people are relegated to carrying out someone else's orders, they are prevented from having a full measure of the opportunity to achieve. They can't get truly inspired about peak performance unless they are shown enough respect to be asked for their input on which goals are most challenging and worthy.

However, organizations led by empowering leaders can reach performance levels unheard of and even undreamed of.

One is too small a number to achieve greatness.
—JOHN C. MAXWELL

Empowering leaders seek input from their employees at the very beginning of the goal-setting process and before defining any team or organization goals. And they do so by:

- MBWA (Management By Walking Around), which is an unstructured manner of walking/wandering through the workplace to talk with employees or inquire about the status of ongoing work.

- Group exercises to brainstorm and facilitate ideas and thoughts.

When you, as the leader, sincerely seek your people's input, better comprehension and dedication is achieved. Goals are more clearly defined, and your team displays a stronger sense of ownership. As employees become involved in the creation, development, and implementation planning stages, they also feel greater satisfaction and accomplishment when the goals are reached.

Even President Kennedy, when he set the goal of placing a man on the moon, emphasized this sense of collaboration and group achievement:

"In a very real sense, it will not be one man going to the moon—if we make this judgment affirmatively, it will be an entire nation. For all of us must work to put him there." He knew it couldn't just be his goal if it was to succeed; it had to be the shared goal of the entire country.

The empowering leader can improve his or her team's performance by understanding the following five benefits of team goal setting. When you involve your people in the goal-setting process, you can:

- Afford you and your team more resources, ideas, and energy than you could as an individual.

- Maximize your team's potential and minimize its weakness. Strengths and weaknesses are more exposed in individuals.

- Better devise several alternatives when teams provide multiple perspectives on how to reach a goal. Individual insight is seldom as broad and deep as that offered by a team when setting goals.

- Share with the team the credit for victories and the blame for losses.

- Simply do more as a team than as an individual.

So do you see how both planning and goal setting occur from the top down *and* the bottom up? It might also be helpful to observe that, in order to get the *power* in em-*power*-ing others to work, it is necessary to recognize the *"we"* within po*we*r.

Pause for Reflection:

1. *Have you surrounded yourself with highly motivated people who form a high-performance team and who have a can-do spirit?*

2. *Would you like to become an empowering leader?*

Goals Have Different Meanings to Different People

Several years ago, my wife and I went to see the Cirque du Soleil show "O" in Las Vegas. As you may know, Cirque du Soleil is a dramatic mix of high-quality, artistic circus acts and street entertainment. Not long after that, I took my oldest grandson to a traditional circus show passing through our hometown. Although both qualified as a trip to the circus, the experiences were vastly different.

What picture comes to your mind first when I say the word "circus"? Do you envision the elephants, the clowns, the trapeze, the lions, or even the cotton candy? Your description would most likely depend on your specific experiences. In a similar way, each of us would likely have different takes on describing the word "goal."

Insight: Two people can describe a word or concept in vastly different ways because of their different life perspectives.

Two Important Questions

Empowering leaders, as well as highly motivated employees who form a high-performance team and have a can-do spirit, will continually revisit two questions:

- What is our goal?
- Are we making progress toward it?

They ask these questions about their long-term strategies, about their tactical efforts, about each meeting they attend, and about process-oriented matters such as their approaches to communication, coordination, and cooperation.

Vaguely Defined Goals Confuse and Frustrate

If I say the word "elephant," you can no doubt clearly picture an elephant. However, what picture comes to mind first when I say the word "goal" or "goals"? You'd need a lot more information, right?

During one-on-one sessions with leaders and with each member of their leadership teams, I usually receive different answers when I ask, "What are your goals?" Just as frequently, the leadership team is not even clear as to what the goal is. That's not good.

When answers are diverse among the leaders and their leadership teams, there is bound to be even greater uncertainty at lower levels in the organizations—and for sure for employees on the front line. Normally, it can be traced to vagueness.

Can people work together as an effective team if they don't have a clear picture of the team's goals? How can they maximize their feelings of achievement if they don't have predetermined goals—the achievement of which is the definition of success? They can't!

A Leader's Responsibility

In order to achieve success with a high-performance team, you must clarify and communicate goals. First, it is the leader's responsibility to effectively communicate the organization's *values* (Who are we?) and *purpose* (Why do we exist?), neither of which ever changes.

Establishing and clarifying your values and purpose facilitates planning, priority setting, and decision making at all levels within the organization. And it creates the opportunity for your people to feel the achievement of fulfilling the organization's values and purpose.

So what is and is not a goal? Second, how do you define the word "goal"?

Since your people come to work with such diverse perspectives, when you say the word "goal," they may think of their own personal goals that they want to accomplish outside of work. However, in an organization, it is the leader's responsibility to clarify and communicate what a goal is. Often, I find that the word "goal" is used loosely in an organization to mean different things to different people at different times and under different circumstances. This vagueness only adds to the confusion.

Eliminate Vagueness!

In my company, as the leader, I was very intentional about clarifying and clearly communicating not only our core values and our purpose but also the differences between our vision, our strategic and tactical plans, and our measurable performance goals.

Here's a quick outline to help you visualize the differences:

Vision Statement:

- Answers the question: "Where do we want to be?"
- Articulates our overarching future direction/dream.
- Can change over time.

Strategic Plans:

- Answer the question: "What do we want to accomplish?"
- Outline our general approach or plan for achieving our goals.
- Serve as our beacon.
- Begin with our goals and work backward to the current status.

Tactical Plans:

- Answer several questions:
  - o "How can we get there?"
  - o "When do we want to arrive?"
  - o "Who can make it happen on schedule?"

- Begin with current status and lay down a path of action steps for implementing strategies.

Measurable Performance Goals:

- Target specific activities.

- Are tied to numeric and timeliness measures of success.

Leading AND Managing

Observation: Usually, the leader's bent is to focus on the vision and strategic plans, whereas the manager's bent is to focus on the tactical plans and measurable performance goals.

As you purpose to eliminate vagueness and work to clearly define and communicate goals, remember that you'll need to recruit the help of both leaders and managers in your organization. Great leaders set the vision, direct the formation of strategic plans, *and* recruit capable managers to help create the best tactical plans and measurable performance goals.

Pause for Reflection:

1. *As the leader of your business, answer this question: What is the goal?*

2. *And are you making progress toward your goal?*

Navigating the Road

On my daily bicycle trips, I usually ride the country roads near our home. Bicycling is an enjoyable way for me to exercise, and it gives me time to think! In fact, a recent ride revealed some powerful insights on leadership.

One day while my wife and I were bicycling, we encountered a one-mile section of road that was full of potholes from recent excessive rains. Normally, my wife likes me to lead the way on this section of road because of my experience in looking ahead and navigating around any obstacles, and this day was no exception as she followed closely behind me. In doing so, I learned two leadership principles:

1. Because she was following so closely behind me, she could not see ahead in order to assess the condition of the road.

Insight: It is the leader's responsibility to know the way, to point the way, and to show the way because followers cannot see ahead.

2. Since she could not see ahead, I needed to clearly communicate where the potholes were.

It is the sender's responsibility to see that the receiver has gotten the message.

—JIM LUNDY

Once the responsible leader of an organization, a division, or a department has clarified and communicated what *a* goal is and what *the* goal is, the next question is, "So what?" The leader has declared the goal. But it takes much more than this.

It all starts from a foundation of *trust*. People will not follow an untrustworthy leader. Next, effective leaders intentionally *connect* with their people and *empower* them with meaningful roles and mutual respect. Finally, as the leader, you are responsible for *navigating* the road ahead. After all, good leaders do more than control the direction in which they and their people travel. They:

- See the whole trip in their mind before moving forward.
- Have a vision for getting to their destination.
- Understand what it will take to get there.
- Know whom they'll need on the team to be successful.
- Recognize the obstacles long before they appear.

A leader is one who sees more than others see, who sees farther than others see, and who sees before others do.

—LEROY EIMS

To be an effective navigating leader requires an ability to balance between:

- Optimism *and* realism.
- Intuition *and* planning.
- Faith *and* fact.

And these leaders have a professional will to find a way for the *team* to succeed because they believe that anything less than success is unacceptable. After all, it is not the size of the goal or project that determines success. It is the size of the leader.

Anyone can steer the ship, but it takes a leader to chart the course.

—JOHN C. MAXWELL

Pause for Reflection:

1. *Are you living out the qualities needed to lead your team to success?*

2. *How much time do you spend charting the course and then clearly communicating what lies ahead to your people?*

Are You a Tour Guide or a Travel Agent?

A few years ago, my wife and I went on a tour of the country of Israel. It was a very enjoyable and educational trip. And one factor was perhaps the main reason for our delightful trip—we had a wonderful tour guide. What made him such a positive influence?

Our tour guide:

- Knew each part of the tour intimately.

- Enjoyed the journey so well that it was fun to hear him share stories and experiences about what we were seeing.

- Inspired us with his passion. We fell more in love with the scenery and archeology because of him.

- Loved the journey. He talked about every part with great energy.

- Was right there on the tour with us when things did not go as planned.

- Had already been where he was taking us and was able to instruct because he was familiar with the journey.

- Spoke from a place of personal authority, so we listened.

- Was quite credible.

From the time we started in the morning to when we made our evening stop at our hotel, he was constantly talking and interpreting what we were seeing. Our trip was immeasurably smoother, safer, and more enjoyable because he made the journey with us.

Many people also utilize the services of *travel agents,* but the outcome is dramatically different. Travel agents:

- Tell you about all the places you could visit, whether or not they have ever been there before.

- Provide you with intellectual information in brochures that describe the sights to see.

- Smile and tell you to have a nice trip.

- Do not go with you.

As you navigate the road ahead, remember that good leaders are much like *tour guides* when it comes to setting the organization's future direction and vision, which determine how and where they and their people will travel.

Their envisioned future is so vivid to them, it is as though they have already taken the journey. And they have come back to take their people up to the mountaintop because they want the *team* to feel and experience the same victorious *dream.*

In fact, it is the leader's responsibility to ensure that the vision for their organization is clearly defined and effectively communicated. A clear vision is a critical component to success. No one said it better than King Solomon:

Where there is no vision, the people perish.

You might be wondering, "How do I actually go about determining my vision?" I'm glad you asked! Like a good tour guide preparing for a trip, an effective leader starts by asking questions, connecting with others, and analyzing the situation.

1. Ask: Where Do You Want To Be?

Before you, as the leader, ask yourself, "Where do we want to be?" you must ask yourself:

- Where have we been?

- Where are we now?

Once you have a firm understanding of the answer to these two questions, it will be time to determine where you want to be in the future.

2. Connect: MBWA

This is another excellent time to connect with your people through MBWA (Management By Walking Around). When you walk and wander through the workplace in an unstructured way, open to the conversations and interactions that spontaneously arise, you will be surprised at the insights you glean and the connections you form. Use the occasion to simply talk with employees or inquire about the status of ongoing work. All of this can be key to forming the complete picture you need for determining your vision.

MBWA should be done by you, the leader, as well as by your leadership team so you all know with certainty what your employees are thinking and what they recommend for quality improvements.

And just as importantly, you want to learn:

- What do your customers want to buy from you?

- Does your organization give your customers what they want?

MBWA is a prime way to connect with your people, and real connection occurs when you win people over before you enlist their help. You, as the leader, have the responsibility of initiating connection with your people.

People don't care how much you know until they know how much you care.

—THEODORE ROOSEVELT

Never underestimate the power of building relationships with your people before asking them to follow you. When the leader has done well to connect with his or her people, you can expect to see employees exhibiting loyalty and a strong work ethic. And the leader's vision becomes an inspiration to the people.

3. Analyze: SWOT

A SWOT (Strengths, Weaknesses, Opportunities, and Threats) analysis is a structured planning method used to find your competitive advantage and to evaluate:

- Internal Factors (inside the organization)

  o Strengths: Characteristics of the business or project that give it an advantage over others.

  o Weaknesses: Characteristics that place the business or project at a disadvantage relative to others.

- External Factors (outside the organization)

  o Opportunities: Elements that the project could exploit to its advantage.

  o Threats: Elements in the environment that could cause trouble for the business or project.

- Note: External factors may include macroeconomic matters, technological changes, legislation, and sociocultural changes, as well as changes in the marketplace (customers and suppliers) or in competitive position.

> So it is said that if you know your enemies and know yourself, you can win a hundred battles without a single loss. If you only know yourself, but not your opponent, you may win or may lose. If you know neither yourself nor your enemy, you will always endanger yourself.

—SUN TZU, *THE ART OF WAR*

Once you have connected with your people, analyzed your organization, and determined where you have been and where you are now, you are in a prime position to clarify your vision for the future. It's now time to take the next step. In the next chapter, we'll learn how to write a vision statement.

Pause for Reflection:

1. *As a leader, do you feel more like a tour guide to your employees or a travel agent?*

2. *What opportunities did you identify in your SWOT analysis?*

CHAPTER ELEVEN:
A Powerful Way to Unite and Inspire Your Team

PERPETUATE YOUR LEADERSHIP BY SETTING GOALS AND MONITORING PROGRESS

"Goals convert vision into energy."

DAVE RAMSEY

W hen Ryan Murphy was eight years old, he gave a handwritten note to his parents that read as follows: "I hope my swimming life continues and I become an Olympian when I grow up. I hope I will break the world records. I want to be the best swimmer in the world. THE END!!!!!" The note featured a drawing he did of himself with a gold medal.

On August 8, 2016, American swimmer Ryan Murphy, now twenty-one, set a new Olympic record in the hundred-meter backstroke at the Summer Olympics in Rio de Janeiro. Oh, and he won that gold medal in the process. Over the next few days, two more races meant two more gold medals, and in his last race of the games he shattered the *world* record for the hundred-me-ter backstroke, becoming the fastest swimmer in history for this event.

He had a vision that drove him through thirteen years of training—a vision worthy of five exclamation points.

Cast Your Vision in Three Simple Steps

What is your destiny? Where will you be in five years? Or ten, or even thirty? Of course, no matter how hard you search, no one can answer that question with absolute certainty.

But I am certain of this: whether you are an Olympic athlete or the lead-er of an organization, the journey toward your destiny always begins with a vision. Vision is the roadmap to your destiny—the picture of your purpose. Without it, you may find yourself off course—or worse, going nowhere. So dream big . . . bigger . . . even bigger, because it is your dream, and the dream you dream will define the life that you live!

You can cast a vision for your organization by following these three simple steps:

1. Thoroughly Understand the Criteria

If you observe the following conditions, you will be prepared to cast an excellent vision statement. Let's first start with what a vision statement is *not:*

- About money (revenue or profit). Money only gets move-ment. Money is not enough to actually motivate your employ-ees. People will work harder for *meaning* than for money.

- Verbose.

- Convoluted and hard to understand.

- Impossible to remember.

Now let's look at what a vision statement is or does:

- Is aligned with your core values and purpose.

- Is vibrant and engaging.

- Is a huge and exhilarating challenge to reach.

- Is clear, compelling, and easy to grasp.

- Is a unifying focal point that galvanizes people.

- Is a catalyst that creates a team spirit as people strive toward it.

- Inspires passion, intensity, emotion, and a conviction for living it out.

- Has a wow factor.

- Is energizing and exciting to a broad base of people, not just the executive team.

- Comes from leaders who are 100 percent committed to it.

2. Vividly Describe Your Vision

So that you and your employees can explain the vision statement to all stakeholders (e.g., employees, customers, suppliers, investors), use words that clearly describe your vision. Vividly describe your envisioned accomplishments as though, fifteen years from now, you have been asked to write an article for an international publication about an award you have received for accomplishing your vision:

- What has been your unique impact on the marketplace?

- What are your customers experiencing? Why are they saying "WOW!" to describe your service?

- What have these achievements meant to your employees? How do they feel?

- What competencies and systems have you developed?

- What are your suppliers saying about your accomplishments? And why?

3. Collaboratively Record Your Vision

As an empowering leader, after you have reviewed the criteria and written a vivid description, you should seek input from your employees at the very beginning of the process for the vision statement and before stating the final version.

By now, these three key questions should come automatically:

1. *Who* can help me write a better vision statement?

2. *Who* will have to carry it out?

3. *Who* will be impacted by it?

The next step is for you, as the leader, to facilitate group exercises and brainstorm two to five short, expressive snippets from the vivid description that you drafted in the exercise above. As with other times, when you sincerely seek your people's input, they will have a better understanding of and commitment to the vision that you collaboratively set. Furthermore, when employees are involved in the creation and development of a clear, concise vision statement, they take pride in the achievement of the vision.

While the vision of every organization is unique, we can sometimes gain a deeper understanding of this concept by learning about another company's vision statement. The vision statement of my moving and storage company was *Revolutionizing the Way People Move*. And we truly lived it out. Just ask about my company's reputation in our industry over the past twenty years.

Two Guiding Super-Objectives for Every Business

Have you ever formed a habit for one reason and then discovered some unexpected "fringe benefits" related to your new habit? Bicycling has been that way for me. I started cycling as a way to get in shape, but that is only one of its many benefits! For many years, I have used my long bicycle rides to:

- Burn calories. I love to eat.

- Reduce stress. As the leader, I had constant challenges and opportunities coming at me.

- Think. I needed time to work *on* my life and family as well as *on* my business.

As much as I appreciate the caloric burn, it is the thinking time that was most valuable to me.

One day while on a long bicycle ride, I was thinking and kept asking myself, "At the end of the day, what do we want to accomplish in our business? And could it be stated simply, so that our people could easily understand and remember it?" It finally came to me that, at the end of the day, we wanted to accomplish only two things:

- Delight Customers.

- Increase Operating Profits.

I later called these our Super-Objectives because they became the two high-level, overarching objectives for our business.

Observation: These Super-Objectives can apply to any and all organizations.

You can successfully achieve your organization's goals by championing these two Super-Objectives.

1. Delight Customers

Over the years, I have concluded that there are three types of customers:

- Unhappy Customers. Their experiences *don't meet* their expectations. The customers feel:

  o   The work was wrong, incomplete, sloppy, or late.

  o   The service provider was rude or unprofessional.

  o   The cost was higher than expected.

- Satisfied Customers. Their experiences *match* what they expected.

- Delighted Customers. Their experiences *exceed* their expectations. The customers feel:

  o   The work was better, more complete, or available sooner than expected.

  o   The service providers were more polite, professional, helpful, or pleasant than expected.

  o   The value (quality and quantity relative to cost) was greater than the customer expected.

In my company, we knew we had *delighted the customer* when we gave them an experience that exceeded their expectations. And we actually had measurable performance goals related to how well we fulfilled our goal to *delight the customer.*

> ## Insight: When you delight your customers, increased operating profits will follow.

2. Increase Operating Profits

Our employees could clearly understand these three simple ways to increase operating profits:

- Increase revenue.

- Decrease expenses.

- Increase productivity.

As the years went by, I, as the owner of the business, became more and more transparent with our company's financial information as we became better at financial forecasting. This transparency was important for two reasons:

- Accountability. The leadership team saw company-wide financial information as well as details strictly relating to their responsible functions (sales, operations, IT, etc.) or business unit (product or service offering).

- Reward. I wanted to share with our people our financial success by awarding bonuses when we performed over and above a certain operating income threshold.

> There is a direct relationship between a leader's transparency about revealing his or her business financial records and the success of that organization. More transparency creates more success!

These two guiding Super-Objectives worked for my company, and they'll work for yours, too. Just remember: if you can delight your customers while increasing profits, you'll see continued success.

Pause for Reflection:

1. *Where do you go when you need to get away and think?*

2. *How could you apply these Super-Objectives in your own organization?*

Laying Bricks or Building Cathedrals?

A great teacher or communicator can use a simple story to convey an important truth. My good friend and mentor Jim Lundy was one such communicator. He would often tell the story about the two bricklayers:

> Both bricklayers were asked what they were doing. The first bricklayer, who worked under an ineffective manager, replied gruffly, "I'm laying bricks." The second, whose supervisor was a communicative leader, looked up with a smile and said, "I'm helping build a cathedral!"

The call to effective leadership exudes from that simple story: What would you like your employees to do? Would you like them to simply help you lay bricks? Or would you like them to enthusiastically help you build cathedrals?

When your people . . .

- Don't know *where* they want to be and

- Are not involved in planning *how* they can get there,

There is . . .

- Little or no meaning or purpose in their work.

- No feeling or recognition of achievement.

Therefore, they feel that they are just "laying bricks."

> ## Observation: Many managers are more comfortable doing today's tasks than planning for the future. Therefore, they tend to jump right to performing tactics before they and their employees know where they are going or where they want to be.

If we're not careful as leaders, our people will think of themselves as merely "brick layers." To lead "cathedral builders," we must be intentional about a few important aspects of our organizations.

It starts when you do your homework to prepare for your vision and continues as you actually craft your vision statement, as we discussed previously. Once you've completed those steps, you are now ready to prepare:

- Strategic plans.
- Tactical plans.
- Measurable performance goals.

These plans are important because the most well-thought-out vision is no good if there are not plans in place for how to achieve that vision. For now, let's focus on strategic plans and tactical plans.

> ## Observation: Quite often, managers confuse strategy and tactics and think the two terms are interchangeable—but they're not. They are separate business functions and practices.

Strategic planning answers two questions:

1. What do we want to accomplish?

2. Why?

Strategic planning is the general approach or plan to achieving your objectives or high-level, desired outcomes. This type of planning paints a picture of the desired future and long-term objectives for where the organization wants to be in three, five, or even ten years. By looking into the future and casting a vision for how to get there, it answers the *why* that motivates your people. Strategic planning begins with the desired end results—the objectives—and works backward to the current status.

To be effective, it must relate to your organization's core purpose: *Why* do you exist? Your leadership team must be involved, but it is a leader's responsibility to communicate, with clarity, the objectives to the total organization. This clarity will help your people to understand what they need to *do* and, maybe even more importantly, what they are *not* to do. It will also enable them to *feel* empowered at the most critically important time of execution.

Here are some examples of strategic plans for my moving and storage company:

- Increase share of market through better understanding and knowledge of market opportunities in order to develop consumer sales.

- Reduce internal and external operating expenses associated with consumer sales.

The strategic plans can be divided by the various product or business lines. For example, in my moving and storage company, we had three lines: consumer, government, and corporate accounts. In addition, the plans can be divided between organizational functions: marketing and sales, operations, IT, finance and accounting, administration (e.g., human resources, legal), and so on.

After you've completed your strategic planning, the next question you need to ask is: How can we get there?

Tactical planning asks:

- *How* can we get there?

- *When* do we want to arrive?

- *Who* can make it happen on schedule?

Tactical planning begins with the current status and lays down a path of action steps for implementing *strategies*. It identifies the courses of actions you will need to achieve those strategic objectives, and it relates to actions taken day to day. As a result, the organization moves forward to achieve the objectives outlined in the strategic plan.

Tactical planning is the responsibility of your front-line people, who are truly the only ones qualified to plan the action steps and perform the work. They know *what* to do, *when* they need to do it, and *how* to do it. And when your front-line people are involved in the decision-making and planning process, they will be inspired to work harder and go the extra mile—whatever it takes to succeed. They will be enthusiastically helping you build cathedrals rather than just laying bricks!

Here are some examples of tactical plans for my moving and storage company:

- "John Doe" in marketing is to create a new post-move consumer survey by September 30.

- "Jane Doe" in human resources is to update the dress code policy by October 31.

Like the strategic plans, the tactical plans can be divided by the various product or business lines and/or by organizational functions.

Strategic and tactical plans are fundamental to the success of any organization. If you fail to do this for your organization, it will be like you are driving a thousand-mile race without a roadmap. If you don't know *where* you want to be or *how* you can get there, then where you end up will most likely *not* be where you hoped. But if you know where you're going and how to get there, your people will help you build a cathedral.

Pause for Reflection:

1. *Are the people you lead laying bricks or building cathedrals?*

2. *Do you have a strategic plan?*

3. *Do you have a tactical plan?*

How to Set Performance Goals That Motivate and Inspire

Over twenty years ago in our moving and storage business, I experienced the true significance of setting measurable performance goals. And I discovered the key to setting performance goals that truly motivate and inspire!

In the local moving division of our business, we asked each individual employee to set some production and quality goals. I was shocked by how well our moving crews rallied behind this request to set measurable performance goals. For example, they set goals for the:

- Number of cartons packed per hour per job.

- Number of pounds loaded per hour per job.

- Number of pounds unloaded per hour per job.

- Cost incurred for cargo claims per job, etc.

Originally, every crew member set goals that were way too high until we gave them feedback on their actual performance. We posted everyone's numbers so they could see how their actual numbers compared to everyone else's. They thought they were doing much better than they actually were.

And they were really surprised that they fell short of *their* goals. Even though we got them to reset more realistic goals, they were so competitive that they did everything possible to beat their current performance numbers.

Insight: If I, as the leader, had set my employees' performance goals, they would not have been surprised at their performance. Their focus would have been directed at me and my goal-setting abilities instead of how they could improve their own performance.

These measurable goals not only helped our moving crews perform better but also helped our leadership team identify which crew members were the most productive (and, more importantly, why they were); which had the lowest cost of cargo claims (and, more importantly, why they did); which needed more training; and which worked best together.

Observation: The employees who had the lowest productivity and the highest cargo claim costs weeded themselves out of our company.

If you want to motivate and inspire your people, help them properly set measurable performance goals. Most organizations will see a dramatic increase in employee performance when:

- A collaborative process takes place between employees and their managers.

- Individual employees effectively set measurable goals that closely tie to the organization's overall strategy.

Like so many things in life and business, setting and advancing toward measurable performance goals is a *process*. What's needed, then, is a way to stay focused on the right things and keep moving in the right direction.

Power Your Purpose

Activity without purpose is like archery without targets.

—JIM LUNDY

In the same way that ambiguous goals are as ineffective as aiming at an invisible target, our activity must align with our greater purpose in order to show results. It is not good enough to simply be busy! Keep asking, "What is our goal?" and "Are we making progress?" This powerful pair of questions can help us keep our activity and our purpose closely intertwined.

How Good Are Your Results?

With numeric and timeliness measures of success, measurable performance goals are your activity targets. These goals always tie back to the strategic and tactical plans to ensure that you profitably reach your customers.

Your measurable goals are set in contrast to past performance and to be obtained over a certain time, such as three months, six months, twelve months, etc. They are set using the *SMART* criteria by asking if they are:

- *S*pecific and vital.
- *M*easurable.
- *A*chievable but challenging.
- Results oriented.
- Time-bound.

Here are some examples of performance goals that are activity targets with numeric and timeliness measures of success:

- Increase sales by 5 percent over same period of last year.

- Increase profit by 2 percent over the average of the prior three months.

- Reduce overtime by 50 percent by the end of the third quarter.

- Increase billable time to 92 percent by the end of the fourth quarter.

When employees measure their progress, stay on track, and reach their target dates, they experience the exhilaration of achievement that spurs them on to continued efforts to reach their goals. People can work together as an effective team when they have a clear picture of the team's goals. And they can maximize their feeling of achievement when they have predetermined goals—the achievement of which is the definition of success!

Pause for Reflection:

1. *What are your goals?*

2. *Are you making progress?*

Identifying Cause and Effect

In 1666, as the story goes, Sir Isaac Newton sat in a garden and came up with the law of gravity after watching an apple fall to the ground (or hit him on the head, depending on which version you believe). The principle suggested by this law is easy enough to understand: gravity pulls, the apple drops. The apple drops, the scientist theorizes.

Cause and effect is a relationship in which one action or event (the cause) makes another event happen (the effect). One cause could have several effects.

The cause is why it happens. To determine a cause, ask, "Why did this happen?"

The effect is what happens. To identify an effect, ask, "What happened?"

There are four criteria that can help us understand this important concept:

- The cause has to occur before the effect.

- Whenever the cause happens, the effect must also occur.

- The strength of the cause also determines the strength of the effect.

- The effect is actually due to *the* cause rather than to some other event or cause.

What are some examples of cause and effect?

Cause: Jump in the pool.

Effect: Get wet.

Cause: You are out of gas.

Effect: Your car won't start.

Cause: You don't submit invoices in a timely manner.

Effect: Your payment comes later than you expected.

Now, you hear a lot these days about companies using "big data" to run their businesses more effectively and efficiently. After attending the School of Hard Knocks for a number of years, I discovered that having the right data is only half of the equation!

Retailers especially are trying to watch changing trends in consumer buying patterns (the cause) so they can respond quickly (the effect). They are using comments made via social media along with other sources and their own data to compare massive and complex amounts of data on how and why customers are changing the buying of products and services.

Over twenty years ago, my moving and storage company set up an internal continuous quality-improvement program. The program proved to be highly successful, which prompted me to ask the following two questions:

- How could we expand our quality program externally to our suppliers? Our suppliers were local moving companies in markets servicing our national long-distance moving business.

- How could we be the best customer our suppliers had ever had?

While asking myself these questions, I remembered hearing complaints from our suppliers that we were not paying them on time. Since we prided ourselves on paying suppliers quickly, I went to our accounting people and asked about the complaints. After they looked into our accounting system, they found all suppliers were being paid as scheduled and on time, per our internal measurable performance goals.

Then I went to our billing people to ask them about the complaints. After they looked into our billing system, they found they were processing the suppliers' invoices as soon as we received them and setting up the payment rather quickly, as defined by that department's measurable goals.

So why were our suppliers complaining? While I was talking with our billing people, one person said that if the suppliers would send in their invoices in a timely manner (the cause), they would be paid faster (the effect). Bingo! We found the cause!

We immediately began to compare the date that suppliers completed their portion of the moving job with the date that we received their invoice. And to our surprise, the gap averaged twenty-eight days. We weren't slow in processing invoices; they were late in sending them to us.

The Solution

Once we started to give our suppliers measurable feedback on the number of days it took for us to receive their invoices, it was amazing how quickly the average number of days came down. Through our measurable feedback, our suppliers found that the slow pay (the effect) was not due to us paying slowly, but that their invoices were just sitting on someone's desk all month waiting to be sent at the end of each month (the cause). They were then able to correct the issues on their end.

This was my first experience in using measurable performance goals to understand cause and effect and in observing how we could use measurable feedback to solve a complaint or problem or even to learn of an opportunity. And I've used it many times since.

I encourage you to put this approach into practice at your own business. I am confident it will produce clear and positive results for you, as it has for me.

Pause for Reflection:

1. *Would you like to be more effective in solving complaints and problems?*

2. *How could you use measurable goals and feedback in your organization?*

Leaders Must Distinguish Symptoms from the Root Cause

It's not always easy to sift through the chaos of a situation—particularly one that's gone off the rails—and determine the contributing factors that brought you to where you are. Symptoms and root causes can look similar on the surface. This is why it's so important to take a deep breath, step back, and evaluate the particulars of the concern. When needed, dig deeper until you discover the root cause.

To walk you through what this looks like in practice, I'm going to share about another experience I had at my moving and storage company. When we set up our continuous quality-improvement program years ago, we found that our ability to distinguish between the symptoms and the actual root cause of a problem was key to the program's effectiveness. Practice and theory are sometimes two different things, so it's my hope that this example will provide a helpful illustration of these concepts in action. Once you start looking, you will find countless opportunities to take similar steps at your own organization.

Complaints Are Opportunities

At that time, I remembered hearing complaints from our suppliers (the local moving companies in markets servicing our national long-distance moving business). They complained that we were *not* consistently picking up the customers' household goods (HHGs) at the residence on the agreed date. This meant that our traditional padded-van truck drivers were *not* arriving on time from out of town to pick up the customers' HHGs at the residence.

The Symptoms

It also meant that those suppliers had to unexpectedly stand in the gap and quickly:

- Pull a moving crew together.
- Put them in a truck.
- Rush them out to the customer's home after they had already performed a full day's work to pick up the customer's HHGs (the *symptom*).

The cost reimbursement for this activity from my company to the supplier really was not adequate compared to their actual cost (the symptom). Then, later that night, the supplier would have to unload their truck and place the HHGs into their storage warehouse (without any reimbursement for storage—another symptom) while waiting for the out-of-town padded-van driver.

This doesn't sound like a highly successful, quality program, does it? If it is true that the shortest route to higher quality in business is to identify and eliminate the root cause barriers to quality, then why was my company having such problems arranging for a padded-van driver to arrive on time and avoid all this "monkey motion" by the supplier?

Solving the mystery of quality improvements can be challenging. And often, we are distracted by the mere symptoms of our problem. There's a simple way to get to the root cause of the problem: by using a technique called "root cause analysis." I used this technique in order to discover why we were having such problems in delivering drivers on time.

Symptom

A symptom is an indicator or sign that a problem exists.

Root Cause

A root cause is the fundamental reason for, or source of, the problem.

Root Cause Analysis

One way to discover the root cause of a problem is to perform a simple root cause analysis. A root cause analysis just requires you to ask a series of *why* questions.

For example, if your employees have low morale, it is a sign of a problem. Low morale doesn't happen by itself, and it can't be resolved by itself.

If you ask, "Why do my employees have low morale?" the answer might be that they are fearful and lack trust in management. If you ask,

"Why are my employees afraid and lack trust?" the answer may be that you have a manager who exhibits destructive behavior. Next, you ask, "Why does my manager exhibit destructive behavior?" and so on.

Each time you can answer the *why* question, you have probably identified a symptom that is actually caused by something else. So continue to ask *why* for each answer until you can no longer generate a logical response. You now have likely reached the root cause that has generated the observed symptoms.

Tip: Once you think you've asked your last "why" question, try to ask "why" one more time. Often, we need to really push through to the end of this process to arrive at the genuine root cause of our problem!

When you have identified the *root cause,* put an action plan in place to solve the problem. Amazingly, many of the *symptoms* will go away as well.

Notice that if you take action too early in the process, you wind up merely addressing the symptoms (often ineffectively). Imagine our scenario of the employees with low morale mentioned above. If you immediately launched a cheery, "Let's get positive!" campaign with your people, you would have missed the root cause of the morale problem altogether!

Twenty years ago, with the type of moving job mentioned above, the customers booked their moving job directly with the supplier, and the supplier would register the customers' moving job with my company.

When we set measurable goals and began to give suppliers measurable feedback, we discovered that when the supplier had to pick up the HHGs at the residence and hold them at their warehouse, the shipment arrived late to its final destination, cargo damage claims increased, and customer satisfaction plummeted. But we also discovered this important symptom: the gap between the customer-agreed pickup date and the date when the suppliers notified us about the pickups averaged only two days! We were finding out about these moves scarcely forty-eight hours before we needed to fulfill them.

Once we started to give our suppliers measurable feedback on the number of days it took for us to receive their registrations, it was amazing how quickly the average number of days significantly increased. This positioned my company to logistically and successfully arrange for a padded-van driver to arrive on time for the customer's agreed pickup date.

The Root Cause

Our suppliers found through our measurable feedback and through a root cause analysis that the missed agreed pickup dates (*symptom*) were *not* due to poor planning on our part but because the customers' booked moving jobs were just sitting on someone's desk waiting—sometimes as much as two weeks—to be registered (the *root cause*).

Using measurable performance goals to understand a root cause and its symptoms enables you to use measurable feedback to solve a complaint or problem or even to learn of an opportunity, which can drive successful financial results for your business. And best of all—the customer wins!

Tip: Use measurable goals and feedback to unemotionally highlight problems and motivate those involved to provide the solutions.

Pause for Reflection:

1. *Would you like to be more effective in solving complaints and problems?*

2. *Are you proactive when it comes to learning about opportunities?*

3. *How could you leverage the power of goals and feedback in your organization?*

4. *Are you using measurable goals and feedback?*

How Business Reviews Can Help Leaders Manage Goals to Results

We've been discussing *goals*. Now let's begin talking about *controls*.

I have learned that as an organization grows, its leaders and leadership *tools* must also grow. I also know the importance of results. Organizations are formed to get results; people are hired to get results; managers and supervisors are recruited and promoted to get results and to assist others to get results.

I think we can agree there is work for us to accomplish and there are goals to be achieved. Results are essential. Once the processes for establishing measurable performance goals have been set, then the process of following up and following through on the goals is needed. These are controls, which require frequent and regular reporting on the progress of goals.

Learn from My Failures

Early in my leadership journey, I tried to manage this "control" aspect of leadership in a very personal way. For many years, I met one on one (almost weekly) with each member of our leadership team to review progress of projects and goals. Even though our business continued to grow, my patience was continually challenged as we reviewed our progress toward achieving our goals with excellence.

My frustrating one-on-one approach lasted until we hired our first chief operating officer (COO) in 2004. One tool he brought into our company was the concept and practice of Business Reviews, and boy, did it make a difference! You can use Business Reviews as a tool for successfully achieving goals and establishing controls by understanding the answers to the following three questions.

1. What is a Business Review?

A Business Review is a monthly forum to drive continual improvements throughout the organization. The basis of a Business Review is to continually revisit two questions: What is our goal (the goal)? And are we making progress (controls)?

This is a simple, open forum for updates, reporting, questions, and discussion. It results in learning, understanding, and action steps that will lead the entire organization toward the desired direction and goals in the most efficient and effective manner.

2. How Does It Work?

Each month, our COO had "the meeting before the meeting" the day before our Business Review with each leadership team member responsible to report. His desire was to help and encourage people to have an excellent presentation regardless of the results (good or not so good) and to avoid any surprises (i.e., red-face moments!).

Here's the breakdown of how a Business Review functioned at my company:

- *Who:* Either the leadership team member or someone from his or her area of responsibility was to do the presentation.

- *What:* Usually, the controller would go first to report the previous month's financial results. This was followed by reporting from the various product and business units (e.g., consumer, government, corporate accounts) and/or organizational functions (e.g., marketing and sales, operations, IT, human resources).

- *When:* The Business Reviews usually occurred around the eighth day of each month, the day after the financials were completed.

- *Where:* They occurred in a room large enough for the attendance of the leadership team and any employee interested in or involved with the presentations.

- *How:* The first couple of times, it took two days to complete the presentations. Then we got it down to one day, and by the time I sold the company in 2011, we held it to half a day. One person electronically recorded any action item assigned to a person for progress reporting at the next Business Review.

3. Why Is It Important?

The emphasis in our Business Reviews was on the progress of our tactical plans. But I continually coached our people on how the progress showed us living out our core values and tied back to our purpose, vision, and strategic objectives.

Business Reviews are *not:*

- Business as usual.

- A time to "shoot the messenger" or spring a "gotcha" on someone.

Tip: Praise in public, and criticize in private.

Business Reviews *do:*

- Use a coaching style as an opportunity to facilitate and motivate progress.

- Create a team-approach culture. We're all in this together.

- Review progress, identify variances in project results and measurable goals, and understand why.

- Take corrective or preventative actions before any goals are missed and adjust timelines or request additional resources, if necessary.

- Expand a project or goal once more information is gathered from other sources.

- Focus people's efforts on the organization's most important goals to execute.

- Strengthen accountability of projects and measurable goals that are visible organization wide.

- Create a culture of continuous, positive change.

- Celebrate and reward people so they will move beyond past accomplishments toward new opportunities, goals, and achievements.

Insight: When each leadership team member was held accountable in front of his or her peers in a Business Review (versus my previous one-on-one sessions), our people quickly achieved significant organization-wide results with excellence.

Business Reviews can help you manage and monitor your people's efforts and accomplishments while reinforcing the top-level objectives and purpose of your organization. In the process, you'll create a highly aligned team that accomplishes more than you ever thought possible!

Pause for Reflection:

1. *Do you have a monthly Business Review process?*
2. *If so, what has been the impact on your organization?*

Seven Communication Opportunities for Every Leader

Concerning real estate, you have heard the phrase, "It's all about location, location, location." Then, may I say that in business, "It's all about communication, communication, communication!"

Successful, values-driven cultures have leaders who consistently offer meaningful communication with a purpose. And they repeatedly communicate internally, with their employees, as well as externally, with customers and suppliers.

Insight: The best leaders see the potential of their people and give them ample information to not only perform in their current positions but also grow into future team members who will accept even more responsibility.

Every employee, at the very least, wants answers to the following four questions:

- Where is the company headed?

- What is my role in this effort?

- How is my performance going to be evaluated?

- How am I doing?

Most leaders know they need to communicate better and more often, but frequently, they don't know how to make it happen, or even what, exactly, they should be communicating regularly! So here's some help.

Effective leaders are continually revisiting two questions (these should be familiar by now):

- What is our goal?

- Are we making progress?

Effective internal communication opportunities are designed to answer these two questions, as well as to:

- Focus employees on their organization's most important objectives and strategies and measurable performance goals.

- Increase understanding of how each person's responsibility aligns and fits with objectives and strategies and measurable goals.

- Strengthen accountability by assigning objectives and strategies and measurable goals that are visible organization wide.

Observation: When you and your people are working together toward the same objectives and strategies, your organization can execute those objectives and strategies faster, with more flexibility and adaptability.

Essentially, your peoples' alignment to the business's objectives and strategies strengthens your leadership and creates an agile organization. People become more engaged with their work.

Insight: People want to pursue something bigger than themselves—something with a purpose that rises above a weekly paycheck or bonus incentive.

Challenge: It's up to the leader to cast the vision and purpose of his or her organization.

Observation: A leader's vision is cast by what he or she says. A vision is also reflected in what is *not* said! In fact, what you don't say communicates as much as what you do say.

Application: If a leader centers communication, recognition, rewards, and attention only around the financial success of the company, the employees will come to understand that the financial "bottom line" is all that matters. Their deep desire to be part of something greater than themselves will either result in ongoing frustration or ultimately draw them away from the organization.

OK, we've established that it is up to the leader to spearhead the communication efforts in an organization, but how does he or she accomplish this important task? I have good news and bad news. First, the bad news: there is no single event or technique that will get the job done. Now for the good news: after years of intentional discovery in this area, I created an effective, multipronged approach that uses seven unique means of communication.

As I outline this approach, I'll use the communication within my company to supply examples, but you will quickly find that each of these seven styles of communication can be readily adapted to your own situation.

1. Friday Stand-Ups

Every Friday at 8:05 a.m., we would ring the cowbell (my favorite part) to have a quick five-to ten-minute, *fun*, informative stand-up meeting to update people on what was going on in the company. For example:

- Let's congratulate John Doe for record sales last week.

- John Doe and his wife had a baby boy last night.

- Jane Doe received a special thank-you from a customer!

- Who can tell us what *Enjoy Change* means?

- Today's door prize goes to _____!

- This afternoon, we will be ordering snow cones for everyone, so be prepared to select your flavor.

- Bobby will be traveling next week to work with customers in Washington, DC, and Florida.

- Remember: Monday, we will start our "Move It and Lose It" weight-loss challenge.

2. MBWA (Management By Walking Around)

By now, you have likely noticed many benefits that result from practicing MBWA. One such benefit is enhanced communication. This unstructured leadership through walking the workplace can lead to illuminating conversations with employees, chances to inquire about the status of ongoing work, and other opportunities to communicate with your team.

Insight: MBWA is *not* when a manager invites an employee into or calls a meeting with a group of employees in his or her office. This is *not* "you come to me" syndrome. MBWA *only* occurs when the leader gets up from the desk and goes out into the people's workspace.

3. Product Line / Functional Meetings

This is a weekly or biweekly meeting, one-on-one or as a team, with a supervisor, designed to review status updates and progress on tactical projects and measurable goals.

4. Business Reviews

A monthly, half-day, comprehensive open forum for the leadership team to give updates by reporting to their *peers* about their progress on tactical projects and measurable goals.

5. State of the Company

My moving and storage company held an hour-and-a-half company-wide "State of the Company" meeting three times a year:

- In early January, after the first of the new year.

- In May, before our peak season.

- In September, after our peak season.

Our COO and I would report our company-wide progress on:

- Where have we been?

- Where are we now?

- Where do we want to be?

6. Executive Team

Key members of our leadership team would usually meet off-site in another city for two half days at least twice a year:

- In spring, before our peak season.

- In August, before our peak season ended.

The purpose of these meetings was to review our progress and brainstorm on long-term, big-picture planning for the future, strategic direction, and the growth of our business.

7. QIC-Days

My company usually held our annual, half-day, company-wide meetings (QIC-Days) in October, after our peak season. The purpose was to emphasize a yearly theme such as "Enjoy Change."

Intentional communication is the only way to ensure alignment between daily work and the overarching core values, purpose, and vision of your organization. When your team's daily efforts are aligned with these overarching cornerstones, you can spend more time defining your strategic objectives and executing on the tactics to achieve them.

Pause for Reflection:

1. *How do you communicate with your people?*

2. *How do you convey where the company is headed and what your team's role is in this effort?*

Tying It All Together

As you develop your capacity as a communicator, you will find opportunities everywhere you look to communicate with your people through use of the other principles explored in this book. In fact, you have likely noticed that all of these strategies overlap and enhance each other in quite a wonderful way. Your leadership will be supercharged when you discover that each principle in this book complements all the others.

You can build your ability to lead *and* manage, to be effective *and* efficient, and to emphasize process *as well as* content—all of this supported by valuing relationships in accord with results. Strengthening one will aid you in strengthening another. In the same way, having an abundance mindset will help you to make principled rather than expedient decisions. As you identify, share, and activate your core values, you will equip yourself for leading effectively with goals and controls. All of this combined will lead—in a powerful, undeniable way—to a winning culture and the success you have only dreamed of.

Keep at it. This is worth it.

CONCLUSION

$\mathbf{A}$s I conclude this book, I am drawn into your heart and mind, fellow leader. Some of the concepts and principles revealed in this book may have been new to you. Many would agree that I have laid out an uncommon path to success. Nonetheless, I have seen these principles transform my own life and the lives of many other leaders.

More importantly, I hope this material serves as a catalyst to transform your leadership, your organization's culture, and, ultimately, the great big world in which we live. People want to be part of something bigger than themselves, and I've learned that to create something big, you have to lead in a special way.

I still remember the day I decided to lead a values-driven company that achieved results rather than a results-driven company that had values. That statement and way of thinking runs counter to the culture of the twenty-first century, but that's not why this day has stuck in my memory; it's because that decision has made all the difference in my life and company. I hope this book has helped bring you to similar moments of clarity on your own path.

I believe the benefits that come from a values-driven approach to leadership present one of the great paradoxes of our time. The power of this approach offers meaning, purpose, and superior results that are "hidden in plain sight" from those who solely chase profits. Keep this in mind when you compare yourself to other businesses that are only out to make a buck—and know that you are taking the wiser course.

As you have no doubt noticed, this is a book of principles. I *love* principles—because once you learn a principle, you can apply it to any number of situations. I believe you will find this to be true as you apply the principles we studied, but also remember that principles are not one and done items—not a checklist to be followed and then set aside as completed. Rather, in order to apply them, you have to *know* them. And deep understanding and knowledge come from repetition of behavior and reflection of thought.

And that is how this simple book can continue to serve you. I urge you to keep returning to it as a guide and source of inspiration. For these principles to come alive, they must be crystal clear in your mind and reflected in your behavior. Your copy of this book, though possibly coffee stained and marked up, will help reinforce the truths contained herein.

Here's another way to effectively absorb and model this information. It's a powerful principle that I've discovered about learning and leading: when you begin to teach others, your *own* understanding grows deeper than otherwise possible. Therefore, one way to truly incorporate these truths into your own life and leadership is to *share them with others.*

Perhaps you'll decide to go through this book with your leadership team. Or you may want to gift it to struggling leaders whom you encounter along the way. Or maybe you'll occasionally email a meaningful quote from the book to those in your circle of influence.

The ways you decide to pass these truths along will vary, but in doing so, you are actually living out one of the main principles in this book. Such sharing can only authentically come from those who embrace the abundance mindset detailed in chapter 5.

We live in such hectic times. Once we finish a task (or book), our minds quickly skip to the next to-do list item or project clamoring for our attention. In such an environment, this book is all but destined to become just another dust-collecting volume on your bookshelf. Before you file it and move to the next thing, please reflect on your current effectiveness. Are your current plans and leadership efforts yielding the results that you desire? If not, could I suggest that you may need to change your approach?

I have found that, when embraced and pursued, the principles contained in this book can form a firm foundation upon which you can build the organization that you desire. And more than a foundation, they provide a framework around which you can love, lead, and grow your people in a structured and sustainable way.

Writing this book has been a labor of love. Any success that I have realized has been firmly rooted in the information and approaches that I've detailed on these pages. And there is no way I could keep these keys to meaningful success to myself.

I am humbled and honored that you invested your valuable time to read this book.

Here we are, at the end. But really, as leaders, we never reach the end. Keep seeking, learning, and growing. A leader always has more to learn.

Until the next chapter,

Bobby

PS: Continue the values-driven journey with me at BobbyAlbert.com.

PPS: Do you want to learn more about your natural inclination toward leading and managing? You can access my free Leadership Identity Assessment at BobbyAlbert.com/LeadershipIdentity.

ACKNOWLEDGEMENTS

I would like to thank all of the people who, over many years, made me look better than I really am:

To Jim Lundy, who was my long-term executive mentor and friend and who took a young, ambitious leader and chipped away the imperfections to make me better.

To Jason Turner, who was our chief operating officer for the Albert Companies. He was the right person, who came at the right time, to take my ideas and turn them into reality.

To Bruce Boyarko, my long-term friend and consultant, who challenged me with his deep thinking and taught me so much about marketing and strategic planning.

To our people of the Albert Companies, each and every one, who gave their all to make our company the best.

To the people at ArcBest Corporation, who acquired my company and made it possible for me to pursue my purpose with passion as I live out my second half of life.

To Brady Beshear, our chief operating officer for my new company, Values-Driven Leadership, who speaks truth in me when I need it and has taken my raw writings and made this manuscript look really good.

To Tim Boswell, the developmental writer who shaped this manuscript into a better representation of my intended message.

To Sissi Haner, whose proofreading skills put the finishing shine on this text.

To the folks at Morgan James Publishing: David Hancock, Aubrey Kosa, my good friend Karen Anderson, and the rest of the team who labored to bring this book into the world.

ABOUT THE AUTHOR

Bobby Albert led the Albert Companies to unprecedented growth—and he did so during one of the most challenging economic periods of our lifetime. His unique leadership, coupled with an unending desire to learn, enabled this CEO and his team to grow revenues, profits, and EBITDA by 500 percent between 2005 and 2011, the year he sold his business to a publicly traded company.

Using the principles found in this book, Bobby created a unique and special workplace culture. The 100 Best Companies to Work for in Texas awarded their coveted designation to the Albert team for the first two years they applied for consideration. A lifelong entrepreneur, Bobby has started twelve different businesses and acquired nine others. His approach to business has been to value people, seek wisdom, embrace humility, and never stop learning.

He is currently president of Values-Driven Leadership, LLC. His passion is to help other leaders build inspiring workplace cultures through values-driven leadership. Bobby writes, speaks, and consults with key leaders to share the principles and practices that he used to grow his company from five employees to an organization of more than 150 team members.

Bobby lives in North Texas with his wife, Susan. They have three married sons and seven grandchildren.

FREE

Online Leadership Identity Assessment Tool

Join hundreds of others who have taken this assessment and use this tool to:

✓ Understand your leadership identity and determine your natural bent toward either leading or managing.

✓ Leverage the inherent strengths and advantages associated with your unique personality.

✓ Identify the areas of growth and advancement available to you, given your leadership identity profile.

✓ Receive feedback and suggested next steps based on your specific assessment profile.

TAKE YOUR FREE ASSESSMENT AT:

BobbyAlbert.com/LeadershipIdentity

IT CAN BE LONELY AT THE TOP

EVERYONE TURNS TO YOU FOR DIRECTION, ADVICE AND LEADERSHIP.

WHERE DO YOU GO FOR GUIDANCE?

If you're a CEO, owner or executive, Bobby can help you:

Identify your most important values to empower your people toward greater meaning and success.

Establish a culture where your employees want to put in the extra effort to get the job done.

Employ proven leadership tools to make better decisions and increase employee engagement.

Adopt specific strategies to guide your team and monitor your progress toward your shared goals.

Are you willing to explore the path to significant personal and professional growth?

START THE CONVERSATION AT:

BobbyAlbert.com/Lead2Grow

MorganJames
Speakers Group

We connect Morgan James published
authors with live and online events
and audiences who will benefit
from their expertise.

Morgan James makes all of our titles available
through the Library for All Charity Organization.

www.LibraryForAll.org

Printed in the USA
CPSIA information can be obtained
at www.ICGtesting.com
JSHW022211140824
68134JS00018B/981